Louisiana Cuisine

with the
Winnons

edited by John Atkins

Dedicated to the Winnon Family

Some like to cook and some don't. The recipes from the ones who like to cook are tried, true, and good. Some are old and have been passed down through the years. Some are by newer cooks. Some are easy and some are more complicated, because some have been around before fast food was ever discovered. We know some of you don't remember that time.

Expression of Appreciation

The compilers of this cookbook would like to thank and express our sincere appreciation to each one who gave so generously of their time and energy in collecting and submitting recipes and assisting with the sale of our cookbooks. Without your help, this book would not have been possible. This is a classic.

ISBN: 978-0-9895790-0-1

CONTENTS

GENEALOGY   2

PRESERVES, PICKLES, DIPS & APPETIZERS   3

SOUPS, SALADS & SAUCES   21

MEATS & MAIN DISHES   45
    Poultry   45
    Beef, Pork, etc.   65
    Seafood   87

VEGETABLES & SIDES   97

BREADS, ROLLS & PASTRIES   109

DESSERTS   123
    Cakes   123
    Brownies, Cookies, etc.   152
    Pies & Cobblers   161
    Custards & Puddings   175
    Miscellaneous   178

SNACKS & BEVERAGES   181

INDEX   193

It's time to dine and watch the Winnons shine.

They searched their repertoires, cupboards, and all their nooks, and came up with this cookbook.

These recipes are tried and proven. Some of these women have had husbands for over forty years, and none have ever had a rib to show. They have always been round and fat.

There are probably more calories between the covers of this book than Carter has liver pills, but who wants to diet when there is food like this around anyway?

It has been said that the way to a man's heart is through his stomach.

So if you are a young woman, or know a young woman who wants to be a good cook, get her one of these cookbooks.

Learn to cook from this book and chefs from all over will want your autograph.

It is a possibility that regular use of this little book could put all restaurants into bankruptcy.

You never know.

Jesse Winnon

Louisiana Cuisine

with the
Winnons

GENEALOGY

Ben & Mary Winnon

Sula & Vivian Colson
Helen (Frost)
Betty Jo

W.T. & Willie
Troy Davis
Otis Davis
Mae (Mardis)
Jesse
George
Steve
Lillian (Atkins)
Rachel

Lynn P & Nannie
Betty Jean (Colson)
Lynn P., Jr./Buddy
Dorothy Gail/Shab (Williams)

Peter P. & Beattie
Bobby Joe
Eddie
June (Dawkins)

James A. & Iva Lou
Jamie (Rawls)
Tommy
Cathy (Bennett)
Randy
Denise (Johnson)
Ronnie
Brian

Elizabeth & Ben Davis
Ben, Jr.

PRESERVES, PICKLES, DIPS & APPETIZERS

FIG JELLY

4 c figs   3 c sugar
1 large pkg strawberry Jell-O,
prepared

Add figs to Jell-O. Mash together with hands. Add sugar and let set one hour. Cook on high heat for 5 minutes, then on low heat for 15 minutes. Store in jars and seal.

Lillian Winnon Atkins

FIG PRESERVES

Figs   6–8 c sugar

Fill a large, heavy pot with figs. Pile high with sugar—amount according to how big your pot is. Cook until figs are transparent and syrup seems a bit thick, about 3–4 hours slow cooking. While these are cooking, gather jars and lids and wash and rinse well. Then sterilize them in hot-hot water. After filling jars, be sure all bubbles are out—run a sterile knife around the inside of the jar. Then make sure rim of jars is clean by wiping with damp paper towel. Top with sterile lids. Be sure they are sealed. As they cool, lid tops will pop.

Mae Winnon Mardis

FIG PRESERVES

From Mildred Swift

4 pounds figs   1 tbsp cream of tartar
1 c Karo   3 lbs sugar
2 c water   1 lemon, sliced thin

Cut tips off fig stems. Wash with hot soda water, using 1 cup of soda to 6 quarts of boiling water. Let stand 15 minutes. Rinse well. Drain. Mix sugar, water, Karo, cream of tartar, and lemon. Let simmer 15 minutes. Add figs. Cook 2 hours. Allow to stand overnight to plump up. Pack in jars and water bath in boiling water for 10 minutes so as not lose any from mold.

Jamie Winnon Rawls

Mayhaw Jelly

4 c mayhaw juice
5 c sugar

1 box Sure-Jell

I add this because it is no longer on instruction sheet in Sure-Jell box, but you can get cooking instructions from the box. Make sure your jars and lids are always sterile.

Makes 3 1/2 pints of jelly
Mae Winnon Mardis

Pear Preserves

I did not know these were so easy until a 92-year-old lady said she has made them like this for years.

1 c sugar for each 2 c pears

Lemons

Cut pieces of lemon and cook with pears and sugar until syrup is consistency desired. Put in hot sterilized jars with lids. Always make sure the top of your jar is clean—wipe with wet paper towel.

Mae Winnon Mardis

Hot Pepper Jelly

3/4 c bell pepper
1/4 c hot pepper or ground red pepper
1 bottle Certo

1 1/2 c cider vinegar
6 1/2 c sugar

Blend or grind peppers finely. Mix peppers, sugar, and vinegar.

Bring to rolling boil. Remove from fire and cool 5 minutes. Add Certo. Mix thoroughly. Pour into jars and seal.

Lillian Winnon Atkins

Pickled Beets

3 c white vinegar
1 c sugar

1 c water
1 tbsp whole cloves

Prepare beets by cutting tops approximately 1 1/2 or 2 inches from the beet. Place in large pot and boil until tender. Slip tops and skin from beets and trim.

Mix and simmer ingredients 10 minutes. Pour over beets that have been cut and packed in sterile jars.

Ivy Gene Winnon

BREAD-AND-BUTTER PICKLES

14 medium cucumbers
9 medium onions
2 hot peppers
1/2 c canning salt
5 c sugar
5 c vinegar
1 1/2 tsp turmeric
2 tsp mustard seed
1 tsp celery seed
1/2 tsp ground cloves

Slice cucumbers and onions thinly. Layer in a pot. Cut up peppers over this and cover with salt. Cover with ice and let stand for 3 hours. Pour off water and add sugar, vinegar, and seasonings. Mix well with hands. Cook until rinds begin to turn brown, but do not boil. Seal in jars while hot.

Yield: About 12 pints
Ivy Gene Winnon

LIME PICKLES

7 lbs cucumbers
(sliced crosswise)
8 c sugar
2 c pickling lime
1 tbsp salt
2 gal water
2 tsp mixed pickling spices
8 c distilled white vinegar,
4–6% acidity

Soak clean cucumbers in water and lime mixture in crockery or enamelware for 12 hours or overnight. Do not use aluminum ware.

Wash 3 times in clean water and soak in fresh ice water for 3 hours.

Combine remaining ingredients and bring to a low boil. Stir until sugar is dissolved. Add cucumbers and soak 5–6 hours or overnight

Boil pickles in soaking liquid for 35 minutes. Fill sterilized quart jars with cucumber slices and pour syrup over cucumbers, leaving 1/2-inch head space. Cap each jar when filled. Process 5 minutes in boiling water bath. Boiling water should cover jars by 1 inch. Start processing time count when filled jars are placed in rolling boiling water. Canner with tight-fitting lid should be left on high heat during processing.

Label. Store in dry, dark, cool place.

Ivy Gene Winnon

" A big oak tree is just a little nut that held its ground."

GARLIC DILL PICKLES

4 lbs 1–2-in cucumbers	7 heads fresh dill
6 tbsp pickling salt	21 peppercorns
3 c vinegar	14 cloves of garlic
3 c water	

Wash cucumbers. Combine salt, vinegar, garlic, and water. Bring pickling liquid to boil. In bottom of sterile jars, put 1 head of dill, 3 peppercorns and, 4 halves of garlic. Pack cucumbers in the pint jars and fill with pickling liquid to 1/2 inch of top. Close jars with lids and place in boiling bath for 10 minutes to seal.

Joyce Atkins Keller

PICKLED EGGS

boiled eggs	salt and pepper (to taste)
sliced onions	crushed red pepper (to taste)
sliced bell peppers	jalapeno peppers (optional)
whole garlic	apple cider vinegar
sugar	water

Boil as many eggs as you think you will need. The amount depends on the amount of jars you want to use. After you peel eggs, put into jars. Place as much bell pepper and onions into jars as you like. Add to each jar 2 cloves garlic, red pepper, salt and pepper, 1 tsp sugar and as many jalapeños as you like to jars. Measure 1 cup vinegar and 2 cups water for each jar of eggs. Boil mixture and fill jars to 1/2 inch of top of jar with hot mixture. Seal and let set for at least 2 weeks. The longer they set the better they taste.

Ivy Gene Hamby Winnon

REFRIGERATOR PICKLES

From Linda's Kitchen

1/2 c white vinegar	4 medium cucumbers
4 tbsp sugar	1 onion
3 tsp salt	1 green pepper (optional)
dash of pepper	

Mix together vinegar, sugar, salt and pepper. Slice cucumbers, onions and peppers. Marinate in vinegar/sugar mixture for several hours. Juice can be reused at least one more time.

Kim Winnon AmRhein

GREEN TOMATO SOY

2 gal green or semi-ripe tomatoes	2 tbsp dry mustard
12 large onions or 1 gal chopped	2 tbsp canning salt (I use1 tbsp)
1 qt vinegar	1 tbsp allspice (whole)
1 qt sugar	1 tbsp whole cloves
2 tbsp black pepper (I use1 tbsp)	1 tbsp red pepper, if desired

Tie whole spices in cheesecloth bag and add to vegetable mixture in large pot. Cook under medium heat stirring often to prevent sticking. Bring to a boil and cook until mixture becomes thick. This recipe from start to finish will take most of the day. Be sure to keep stirred to prevent sticking—if mixture scorches, it is ruined. Place in sterilized jars and seal with hot lids.

Good with peas, beans, and other vegetables.

Passed down from my grandmother Hamby.

Ivy Gene Hamby Winnon

PICKLED SHRIMP

2 lb raw shrimp	1 1/2 c sugar
2 medium onions, sliced into rings	1 1/2 tsp salt
1 1/2 c vegetable oil	1 1/2 tsp celery seed
1 1/2 c white vinegar	4 tbsp capers with juice

Boil shrimp as usual and peel them. Chill. Make alternate layers of shrimp and onion rings in a sealable container. Mix remaining ingredients and pour over shrimp. Seal and refrigerate 12 hours or more, shaking occasionally. Remove from marinade and serve. I like to double or triple recipe and place in large jar (or trifle bowl) and just let guests eat out of jar. It's very pretty this way.

Gail Winnon Williams

LAYERED SHRIMP DIP

1 3-oz pkg cream cheese, softened

6 tbsp salsa, divided

1/2 c cocktail sauce

3 6-oz cans small shrimp, rinsed and drained

1 2 1/2-oz can sliced ripe olives, drained

1 c (4 oz) shredded Monterey Jack cheese

1 c (4 oz) shredded cheddar cheese

sliced green onions

Combine cream cheese and 3 tbsp salsa; spread into ungreased 9-inch pie plate. Combine cocktail sauce and remaining salsa. Spread over cream cheese. Place shrimp evenly over top; sprinkle with olives. Combine cheeses; sprinkle over olives. Top with onions; chill. Serve with tortilla chips.

Donna Winnon Cox

LAYERED BEAN DIP

1 31-oz can refried beans

1 4-oz can chopped green chilies, drained

1 envelope taco seasoning mix

2 ripe avocados, peeled and pitted

2 tbsp lemon juice

1 1/2 c sour cream

1 jar taco sauce

1 1/2 c (6 oz) shredded cheddar cheese

1 4-oz can black olives, sliced

3 c shredded lettuce

tortilla chips

Mix together refried beans, green chilies and taco seasoning mix. Spread on a 12-in round serving platter. Blend avocados, lemon juice and 1/2 cup taco sauce until smooth. Spread on top of bean mixture. Spread sour cream on top of avocado mixture. Top with lettuce, cheese, taco sauce and olive slices. Serve with chips.

Merri (Cissie) Winnon Rushing

BUFFALO CHICKEN WING DIP

Wings without the bones! Great for football parties. I never have any left!

1 lb skinless, boneless chicken breasts

1 8-oz bottle ranch dressing

1 16-oz package shredded cheddar cheese

2 8-oz packages cream cheese, softened

1 12-oz bottle hot pepper sauce

Preheat oven to 350°F.

Boil chicken breasts until done. Cool and shred chicken.

Pour the ranch dressing, cream cheese, and wing sauce into a bowl and mix until combined. Add the shredded chicken and mix well. Spread the mixture into a 9x13-inch baking dish. Sprinkle the cheddar cheese over the top.

Bake in a preheated oven until the cheese is bubbling (about 10 min).

Serve with heavy crackers or Pita Chips.

> Note: I also cook this in the crockpot . . . just all ingredients together, and cook on low.

Kimberly Winnon AmRhein

HOT CRAB DIP

2 8-oz pkgs Philadelphia cream cheese, softened	2 tbsp dry white wine
2 6-oz cans crabmeat, drained and flaked	1 tbsp Kraft Horseradish sauce
1/4 c sliced green onions	1 tsp hot pepper sauce

Preheat oven to 350°F. Mix all ingredients with electric mixer (on medium speed) until well blended. Spoon into 9-inch pie plate or quiche dish. Bake 25–30 minutes until lightly brown. Serve with crackers or chips.

Merri (Cissie) Winnon Rushing

MEXICAN DIP

2 8-oz pkg cream cheese, softened	2 cans Ro-Tel
1 lb Jimmy Dean Hot Sausage	

Crumble, brown, and drain sausage. Add cream cheese and Ro-Tel. Serve warm.

Merri (Cissie) Winnon Rushing

LAYERED MEXICAN DIP

3 medium ripe avocados	2 10-oz cans jalapeno bean dip
3 tbsp lemon juice	1 large bunch green onions, chopped
1/2 tsp salt	3 medium tomatoes, chopped
1/4 tsp pepper	2 3 1/2-oz cans sliced black olives
1 c sour cream	jalapeño peppers, sliced
1/2 c mayonnaise	1/2 lb shredded sharp cheddar
1 pkg taco seasoning mix	1/2 lb shredded Monterey Jack

Layer 1. Peel, pit and smash avocados, add lemon juice, salt and pepper in bowl.

Layer 2. Combine sour cream, mayonnaise and taco seasoning in another bowl. Spread bean dip on bottom of serving dish.

Add layer 1, then add layer 2. Sprinkle with green onions, olives, diced tomatoes, and jalapeño peppers and cover with cheeses. Refrigerate (I make the day before).

This is my best composite of all the Mexican dips I've made through the years and if there is a family gathering where Jason Colson will be there, this has to be waiting for him.

Gail Winnon Williams

CILANTRO DIP

2 4-oz cans chopped black olives

2 4-oz cans chopped green chilies

1 8-oz bottle Italian dressing

8 oz Monterey Jack cheese, grated

8 chopped green onions

2 chopped tomatoes

1/4 c chopped fresh cilantro

1 6-oz can tomato sauce

Mix all ingredients together. Chill. Serve with tortilla chips.

Merri (Cissie) Winnon Rushing

CILANTRO DIP

2 cans (3–4oz) chopped black olives

2 cans (3–4oz) chopped green chilies

1 8-oz bottle Wishbone Italian Salad dressing

8 green onions, chopped

2 chopped tomatoes

4 oz Monterrey Jack cheese, grated

1/4 c fresh cilantro, chopped

Mix and chill. Serve with chips.

Merri (Cissie) Winnon Rushing

CORN DIP

1/2 stick margarine

1 tbsp sliced pickled jalapeno peppers

1 tbsp pepper juice

2 8-oz pkg cream cheese

3 cans white shoe peg corn, drained

1 tsp garlic powder

salt

Tony's seasoning (to taste)

Mix all ingredients together thoroughly. Chill 1–2 hours. Serve with corn chips or tortilla chips.

Merri (Cissie) Winnon Rushing

CRAWFISH DIP

1 lb crawfish tail	1 onion, chopped
1 lb bulk sausage (may use hot)	1 bell pepper, chopped
1 can cream of mushroom soup	1 tsp Creole seasoning (Tony's)
1 lb Mexican style Velveeta	1 tsp chili powder

Brown sausage and drain. (I usually cook onions and bell pepper while browning the sausage.) Melt soup and Velveeta; add sausage and crawfish and seasonings. Simmer until well blended. Heat through.

Serve as dip with chips or over cooked rice.

Marilyn S Winnon (Buddy)

CHICKEN ENCHILADA DIP

1 c (8 oz) mayonnaise	1 4-oz can diced green chili peppers
8 oz shredded cheddar cheese	1 jalapeño pepper, finely diced

Preheat oven to 350°F.

Place all ingredients in a medium-sized bowl and mix well.

Transfer to a medium-sized baking dish and bake uncovered in preheated oven for 30 minutes or until bubbly and the edges begin to brown.

Marilyn S Winnon (Buddy)

MAE'S MAXIMS

" He hath shewed thee, o man, what is good, and what doeth the Lord require of thee, but do justly, and to love mercy, and to walk humbly with thy God." – Micah 6:8

Salsa Dip

2 large tomatoes, chopped

4 green onion, chopped

1 small can chopped green chilies

1 small can sliced black olives

1 jalapeño pepper

1 tsp each salt, pepper, garlic salt

3 tbsp vegetable oil

3 tbsp vinegar

Mix well, chill before serving. This keeps well for several days.

Jamie Rawls

Salsa

4 large cans whole tomatoes, chopped

4 c 5% vinegar (1 c per each can tomatoes)

4 large onions, chopped

2 lb jalapeño peppers (about 10), with seeds

1 tbsp oregano

4 tbsp garlic (one tbsp per each can of tomatoes)

2 bunches cilantro, chopped (no stems)

1 heaping tbsp cumin

2 tbsp salt

Bring all ingredients to boil. Turn down heat and simmer for 10 minutes. May be frozen or canned in jars for storage. Add hot mixture to cleaned pint jars; then add lids and rings; make sure lids "pop" to ensure they are sealed.

Merri (Cissie) Winnon Rushing

Salsa

1/2 c white sugar

7 tbsp brown sugar

dash of cumin

1 small can tomato paste

1 clove minced garlic

1 green pepper, finely chopped

1 onion, finely chopped

8–10 tomatoes, skinned and roughly chopped

Mix together in large pan. Simmer slowly for 2–3 hours until the salsa cooks down.

Joyce Atkins Keller

SPINACH-ARTICHOKE DIP

1 10-oz pkg frozen chopped spinach, thawed

1 14-oz jar artichoke hearts, drained and quartered

1 5 1/2-oz container garlic-herb soft spreadable cheese (Alouette)

1 c shredded Parmesan cheese

1 8-oz container sour cream

1/2 c mayonnaise

1 2-oz jar chopped pimento (drained)

6 slices bacon, cooked & crumbled

Drain spinach well (squeeze between paper towels). Stir spinach and next 6 ingredients together. Spoon into a lightly greased 11x7-inch baking dish. Bake at 400°F for 20 minutes or until bubbly. Sprinkle with bacon.

Merri (Cissie) Winnon Rushing

DIPPING OIL FOR ITALIAN BREAD

1 env Good Seasons Italian Salad Dressing & Recipe Mix

1/2 c extra virgin olive oil

1 loaf French bread

Mix salad dressing mix and oil in shallow serving bowl. Cut bread into 1-inch slices. Serve bread as dipper for oil mix.

Merri (Cissie) Winnon Rushing

FRUIT DIP

1 jar marshmallow cream

1 pkg cream cheese

Mix thoroughly. Serve with sliced apples or fruit of choice.

Merri (Cissie) Winnon Rushing

APPLE DIP

8 oz cream cheese, softened

3/4 c brown sugar

3/4 c granulated sugar

1 tsp vanilla

Mix well and serve with sliced green apples or other fruit.

Mae Winnon Mardis

SHRIMP SPREAD

1 can shrimp, drained

1 8-oz pkg cream cheese

1 bottle Crosse Blackwell Cocktail Sauce

Put block cream cheese on dish. Flatten until about 1/2 inch thick. Cover with shrimp. Pat so shrimp will stay in place. Pour cocktail sauce evenly over shrimp. Refrigerate. Serve with crackers.

Jamie Winnon Rawls

CHEESE BALL

2 8-oz pkg cream cheese	2 c pecans, chopped
1/4 c green (bell) pepper finely chopped	1 tsp seasoning salt
2 tbsp finely chopped onions	1 8-oz can crushed pineapple, drained

Mix cream cheese, onions, peppers, pineapple and 1 c pecans. Shape into roll on wax paper. Roll formed rolls in chopped pecans until well coated. Refrigerate 1–2 hours. Serve with crackers or chips.

Merri (Cissie) Winnon Rushing

CHEESE BALL

2 8-oz pkg cream cheese	1 small can chopped black olives
1 tbsp mayonnaise	1 jar chopped mushrooms
1 bundle chopped green onions	

Mix all ingredients together with softened cream cheese. Form into ball. Chill for about 1 hour. Roll in finely chopped pecans.

Brenda Winnon Myers

WORD OF GRACE CHEESE BALL

2 8-oz pkg cream cheese	1 tbsp Worcestershire sauce
2 c shredded cheddar cheese	1 tbsp lemon juice
1 c Sharp white cheddar cheese (optional)	2 tbsp finely chopped green onions
1 c medium cheddar cheese	1 tbsp garlic salt
2 tbsp green pepper, chopped fine	paprika
2 tbsp pimento, chopped fine	pecans, finely chopped

Mix all ingredients except paprika and pecans, well. Shape into a ball or rolls 1 1/2 inch round. Sprinkle with paprika or roll in chopped pecans. Chill. Serve.

Jamie Winnon Rawls

JAMIE'S CHEESE BALL

2 8-oz pkg cream cheese
1 small can crushed pineapple
1 small jar pimento
2 tbsp seasoned salt
crushed pecans

1 tsp garlic salt or powder
2 c grated cheddar cheese
3 tbsp bell pepper
2 tbsp green onion

Drain pineapple through paper towel. Mix together. Roll in pecans and chill. Enjoy!

Jamie Winnon Rawls

SAUSAGE BALLS

1 lb cheddar cheese, grated
1 lb hot pan sausage

2 c Bisquick Mix

Cook sausage and drain off grease. Add grated cheese and Bisquick mix. Roll in small balls. Place on cookie sheet and bake at 400°F about 10 minutes until brown.

Mae Winnon Mardis

SAUSAGE BALLS

3 1/2 c Bisquick or
Pioneer Biscuit Mix
12 oz Velveeta, crumbled

1 jar jalapeño peppers, diced
(may use less if desired)
1 lb hot ground sausage

Mix the above until well blended. Roll into balls. Place on cookie sheet. Bake at 350°F for 20–30 minutes.

Merri (Cissie) Winnon Rushing

SHRIMP BALL

1 8-oz pkg cream cheese
1 can medium shrimp, drained
1/2 c chopped pecans

1/2 tsp minced onions
1/2 tsp seasoned salt

Mince shrimp and combine with the cream cheese. Add onion and salt. Roll the mixture in the chopped pecans. Serve with crackers.

Ivy Gene Hamby Winnon

POPCORN BALLS

Good, good. Do not double recipe—it is better to make several small batches.

1 c sugar	1/2 tsp salt
1/2 c white corn syrup	1 tsp vinegar
1/2 c water	1 tsp vanilla
1/4 c butter	3 qts popped corn

Combine sugar, syrup, water, butter, vinegar, and salt. Cook, stirring until sugar is dissolved. Continue cooking without stirring until syrup reaches 270°F or forms a brittle ball when dropped into cold water. Add vanilla. Pour syrup over popcorn. Stir until corn is covered. Grease hands. Shape into balls.

Makes 12 balls
Brenda Winnon Myers

COCKTAIL MEATBALLS

1 lb ground beef	1/3 c chopped onion
1 egg, slightly beaten	2 tbsp bread crumbs
1/2 tsp salt	

SAUCE

2 lbs oleo	1 can tomato soup or bar-b-q sauce
2 tbsp brown sugar	4 tbsp Worcestershire sauce
1 tbsp mustard	1 tbsp vinegar

Mix first 4 ingredients and shape into balls. Place in shallow pan and broil until brown. Mix sauce. Cook onion in oleo until tender. Stir in remaining ingredients. Pour over meatballs. Cover. Bake at 350°F for 20 minutes.

Lillian Winnon Atkins

MAE'S MAXIMS

"You don't drown by falling in the water. You drown by staying there. If you are in a difficult situation, don't wear yourself out treading water—start moving toward the shore."

COCKTAIL MEATBALLS

1 lb hamburger meat
1 egg
1 slice stale bun

1 tsp salt
1 tsp Italian seasoning
olive oil

Make meatballs and brown in olive oil. Add to sauce. Heat well.

SAUCE

1 c ketchup
1 tbsp mustard
1 tbsp vinegar
1 1/2 tbsp brown sugar

1/4 tsp Worcestershire sauce
1/2 tsp hot sauce
1/2 c red wine

Combine all ingredients and add to meatballs.

Jamie Winnon Rawls

TEX-MEX ROLLUPS

2 8-oz pkg cream cheese, softened
1 small can chopped green chilies
1 small can chopped black olives
2–3 green onions, chopped
1 pkg large tortillas

1 pkg gourmet shredded cheddar cheese
3–4 dashes Panola
1/2 tsp Worcestershire sauce
garlic salt and Tony's Seasoning to taste

Mix all of the above except tortillas. Spread thin layer on tortilla; roll up as tightly as possible. Continue, using all the tortillas and mixture. Place in Tupperware container overnight. Slice and serve with picante sauce.

Jamie Winnon Rawls

LITTLE SMOKIES

1 pkg cocktail sausages

1 bottle good bar-b-que sauce

In a crockpot put package of cocktail sausages. Add bar-b-que sauce. Heat well.

Jamie Winnon Rawls

POLISH MISTAKES

1 lb hamburger

1 lb sausage

1 lb Cheez Whiz

2 tbsp Italian seasoning

2 lb party rye bread

olives to garnish

Brown hamburger and sausage; drain well. Add cheese and seasoning. Melt over low heat. Spoon onto slices of bread. Garnish. Place on cookie sheet and bake at 350°F for 6–8 minutes.

Note: For a different taste use Mexican Velveeta or add chopped onions to the meat mixture while browning. These can be made ahead and frozen on cookie sheets (do not cook until ready to use). When frozen put in Ziploc bags.

Mae Winnon Mardis

HAM ROLL-UPS

1 large cream cheese, softened

1/3 c mayonnaise

1 tbsp Deluxe Special seasoning

2/3 c pecans, blended

garlic and red pepper to taste

10 slices thin ham

Mix first 5 ingredients and spread on ham slices. Roll up lengthwise, and chill. Slice rolls crosswise in small pieces before serving.

Mae Winnon Mardis

PARTY CRACKERS

1 stick pure butter

1 stick oleo

pecans chopped fine

1/2 c sugar

1 box Waverly crackers

Combine first 3 ingredients in saucepan. Boil for 2 minutes. Spread on crackers. Arrange on platter and sprinkle with chopped pecans. Bake in oven at 350°F for 10 minutes.

Mae Winnon Mardis

PARCHED PEANUTS

2 lbs raw peanuts (medium size)

Heat oven to 450°F. Put peanuts in baking pan and put in hot oven for 5 minutes. Stir. Turn oven off and let peanuts set in hot oven for 1 hour. Perfect every time.

Jamie Winnon Rawls

TOASTED PECANS

3 c pecan halves
4 tbsp butter

salt to taste

Spread pecans in large shallow pan. Melt butter and coat pecans well. Salt to taste. Bake 30-45 minutes in 300°F oven, stirring often. Cool on paper towels.

Jamie Winnon Rawls

CHEX PARTY MIX

3 c Corn Chex cereal
3 c Rice Chex cereal
3 c Wheat Chex cereal
1 c mixed nuts
1 c bite-size pretzels
1 c garlic-flavor bite-size bagel chips, or regular-size bagel chips, broken into 1-in pieces

6 tbsp butter or margarine
2 tbsp Worcestershire sauce
1 1/2 tbsp seasoned salt
3/4 tsp garlic powder
1/2 tsp onion powder

Jacque Winnon Burchfield

HONEY-GLAZED SNACK MIX

This recipe is good when there has been a good pecan crop otherwise it may be quite expensive.

8 c Crispix cereal
3 c mini pretzels
1/2 jar honey

2 c pecans
2/3 c margarine

In large bowl, combine cereal, pretzels, and pecans. In a small bowl place butter and honey and microwave about 2 minutes or until butter is completely melted. Mix well and pour over cereal mixture and stir to coat well. Spread into two greased 15x10-inch baking pans.

Bake at 350°F for 12–15 minutes or until slightly coated. Stir occasionally. Remove from pan and spread on waxed paper to cool completely. Store in air-tight container or gallon Ziploc bag.

Makes about 12 cups
Mae Winnon Mardis

How to Knit a Dish Rag
*Size 8 needles
*100% yarn

Cast 4 stitches on needle. Knit off that needle (K1) then yarn-over (YO) knit next stitches until all are off and on other needle. Turn, K1, then YO to end. Continue knitting each row until you have about 40 stitches. Then you begin to decrease each row.

K1 then K2 together and continue across to end. Turn and continue on until 4 stitches remain on needle in cast off to end. You will have a little square dish rag.

To cast off, knit 1, knit 1.

Pick up a little kit at Wal-Mart called " I Taught Myself to Knit".

If at first you don't succeed, try try again. I was 75 years old when I learned and just love knitting now. So don't give up.

Just call me and I'll help you.

SOUPS, SALADS & SAUCES

3-BEAN SOUP

1/2 lb dried pinto beans

1/4 c baby lima beans

1/4 c great northern beans

2 stalks chopped celery

1 medium onion, chopped

1/4 c chopped bell pepper

1 jar canned tomatoes

1/2 lb sliced pork sausage

1 tsp dry mustard

1 tsp seasoned pepper

1 c leftover ham (optional)

1/4 lb bacon, diced

1 clove garlic

Soak beans overnight in water. Cook beans 30–45 minutes on low heat.

Cook bacon and sausage. When brown, add vegetables and sauté until onion is clear.

Add this mixture to the cooked beans. Salt and pepper to taste. Slow-cook for 3–4 hours until beans are tender.

Jamie Winnon Rawls

BROCCOLI SOUP

1 stick butter

1 c chopped green onions

1 qt milk

1 lb Velveeta cheese

1 can Ro-Tel tomatoes

1 roll garlic cheese

1 roll jalapeno cheese

3 boxes frozen broccoli or 1 bag frozen broccoli (cooked)

3 cans cream of chicken soup

Sauté onions in butter until tender. Melt all cheese in milk slowly over medium heat. Add broccoli, soup and Ro-Tel tomatoes. Add milk to them if needed. Cook for 30–40 minutes over medium heat.

Merri (Cissie) Winnon Rushing

CABBAGE AND BEEF SOUP

From Pam Chambers

1 lb lean ground beef

1/2 tsp garlic salt

1/2 tsp garlic powder

1/2 tsp pepper

2 stalks celery, chopped (can use small amount celery seed instead)

1 16-oz can kidney beans, undrained

1/2 medium head cabbage (or whole small head)

1 28-oz can tomatoes, chopped

1 tomato can water

4 beef bullion cubes

Brown beef in Dutch oven or electric pot. Drain. Add all other ingredients. Bring to boil. Lower heat and simmer covered for 2–3 hours. Will freeze well.

Donna Winnon Cox

CANADIAN CHEESE SOUP

1/4 c butter

1/2 c finely diced onion

1/2 c finely diced carrots

1/2 c finely diced celery

1/4 c flour

2 tbsp finely chopped parsley flakes (fresh or dried)

1 1/2 tbsp cornstarch

1 qt chicken stock

1 qt milk or half and half

1/8 tsp baking soda

1 c processed cheddar cheese, grated (I use Velveeta)

Melt butter in pot in which you plan to cook soup. Add onion, carrots and celery. Sauté until soft. Add flour and cornstarch; cook until bubbly. Add stock and milk, stirring until a smooth sauce is formed. Add soda and grated cheese. Season with salt and pepper. Let simmer a few minutes until well blended. Add parsley a few minutes before serving.

Jamie Winnon Rawls

CHICKEN NOODLE SOUP

1 small chicken, boiled and deboned

1 onion, grated in food processor

1 c carrots, grated in food processor

1 or 2 small potatoes, cubed

2 quarts chicken broth (from cooked chicken)

1/4 c flour

1 c thin egg noodles

Add vegetables to broth and cook over medium heat for approximately 30 minutes or until tender. Add chicken that has been cut in small pieces and coated with flour. Cook 20 minutes longer. Add egg noodles. Cook 6 or 7 minutes longer. Let set for 30–40 minutes for flavor to blend.

Jamie Winnon Rawls

DUCK AND WILD RICE SOUP

1 duck	4 tbsp butter
2 carrots, chopped	4 tbsp flour
1 large onion, chopped	1 c half and half
4 stalks celery, chopped	1 c wild rice, uncooked
5 c chicken broth	

Boil duck in water seasoned with salt and pepper. Cool and debone. Pull meat into bite sized pieces.

Prepare the wild rice in 2 1/2 cups of chicken broth. Meanwhile, melt butter in heavy sauté pan. Add carrots, onion, and celery. Sauté until vegetables begin to brown. Add the flour and mix until flour is incorporated. Slowly add 2 1/2 cups chicken broth and cook until thickened. Stir in the wild rice, meat and, half and half. Simmer until hot. If broth is too thick, add more chicken broth. Season with salt and pepper and serve.

Joyce Atkins Keller

KANSAS CITY PLAZA III SOUP

1 stick butter	1 1/2 c leftover steak
1 c flour	1 c frozen mixed vegetables
1 c carrots	1 303 can tomato
1 c celery	2 tbsp beef base
1 c onion	8 c water

Cube vegetables in 1/2-inch lengths and parboil. Prepare roux with butter and flour. Add to vegetable parboiled in 8 cups water and leftover steak, then remaining ingredients, and bring to a boil. Simmer till done.

Important: Do not salt for beef base—may be salty (taste first).
Add coarse ground pepper to taste.

Gail Winnon Williams

AU GRATIN POTATO SOUP

Really, really good. Enjoy.

1 box potatoes au gratin

3 c water

2 c Ro-Tel tomatoes
w/ peppers

1 c whole kernel corn

2 c milk

2 c shredded cheddar cheese

Mix potatoes au gratin and water together with seasoning packet. Cook until potatoes are tender. Add tomatoes, corn and milk. Heat until warm throughout. Add cheese. Simmer until cheese is melted.

Jamie Winnon Rawls

DELICIOUS HAM AND POTATO SOUP

$3^1/2$ c potatoes,
peeled and diced

$1/3$ c celery, diced

$1/3$ c onion, finely chopped

$3/4$ c cooked ham, diced

$3^1/4$ c water

2 tbsp chicken bouillon

$1/2$ tsp salt or to taste

1 tsp ground white or black
pepper, or to taste

5 tbsp butter

5 tbsp plain flour

2 c milk

Combine the potatoes, onion, ham, and water in a stockpot. Bring to a boil, then cook over medium heat until potatoes are tender, about 10–15 min. Stir in the chicken bouillon, salt, and pepper.

In a separate saucepan, melt butter over medium-low heat. Whisk in flour with a fork and cook, stirring constantly until thick—about 1 minute. Slowly stir in milk, as not to allow lumps to form, until all of the milk has been added. Continue stirring over medium-low heat until thick—about 4–5 minutes.

Stir the milk mixture into the stockpot and cook soup until heated through. Serve immediately.

> *Note:* I added diced carrots and Mexican Velveeta cheese before it was done . . . very good.

8 servings
Joan Winnon

TOMATO SOUP

$2^1/2$ c canned tomatoes

$1/2$ c onion, chopped

$1/2$ c celery, chopped

2 tbsp butter

2 tsp flour

2 c beef stock

$1/2$ tsp sugar

$1/8$ tsp paprika

salt

pepper

Combine first 3 ingredients in pan. Cover and simmer for 15 minutes. Mix flour and butter together and add to the pot. Stir in beef stock and seasonings. Bring to boil and cook until slightly thickened. Season with salt and pepper

Joyce Atkins Keller

TOMATO BISQUE SOUP

1/2 pound butter	1 tsp basil
1 c chopped celery	1 bay leaf
1 c chopped onion	1/2 tsp paprika
1/2 c carrots	4 c chicken broth
1/3 c flour	1/4 tsp white pepper
2 1-lb cans whole Italian plum tomatoes, drained & chopped	salt to taste
2 tsp sugar	2 c whipping cream
1 tsp marjoram (or summer savory)	

Melt butter and sauté vegetables until tender. Stir in flour. Cook 2 minutes, stirring constantly. Add tomatoes, sugar, herbs, and chicken broth. Cook 30 minutes, stirring constantly. Discard bay leaf. Purée soup. Add other ingredients. Can be served hot or cold. May be frozen.

Yield: 8 servings
Jamie Winnon Rawls

TACO SOUP

1 lb ground beef	1 can pinto beans
1 onion, chopped	1 can ranch style beans
1 can Ro-Tel tomatoes	2 cans water (rinse tomato cans)
1 can stewed tomatoes	1 pkg Original Buttermilk Dressing mix (dry)
1 can whole corn (I use frozen corn)	1 pkg taco seasoning

Brown beef, add onion, sauté until onion is clear. Add rest of ingredients and simmer for about 45 minutes or until well seasoned. Serve with cornbread, crackers, or Doritos chips.

Jamie Winnon Rawls

TACO SOUP

2 lbs hamburger

1 small onion

1/2 tsp black pepper

1 1/4 pkg taco seasoning

1/2 c water

1 pkg dry ranch dressing

1 can whole kernel corn with juice

3 cans stewed tomatoes

2 cans pinto beans with juice

Brown hamburger meat. Mix all other ingredients and simmer for 30 minutes.

Brenda Winnon Myers

TEXAS TWO-STEP SOUP IN A JAR

1 1.61-oz pkg Pioneer Brown Gravy mix

2 tbsp mild red chili powder

2 tsp dried oregano leaves

1 tsp ground cumin

1 tsp garlic salt

1–12 regular size tortilla chips, coarsely crushed

1 1/4 c uncooked small to medium size pasta (such as wheels, shells or macaroni)

Pour gravy mix into wide mouth pint jar. In small bowl, stir together chili powder, oregano, cumin, onion and garlic salt. Pour into jar to make second layer. Add layers of tortilla chips and pasta to fill jar. Seal with lid. Attach gift tag (below) and decorate as desired.

GIFT TAG

Brown 1/2 pound ground beef in a large saucepan or Dutch oven. Add contents of jar and 7 cups water. (I added some beef bouillon). Heat to boiling. Stir in 1 can (15 oz) corn with red and green bell peppers and 1 can (16 oz) chopped tomatoes. Reduce heat, cover and simmer for 20–25 minutes or until pasta is tender, stirring occasionally. Serve with crushed tortilla chips and shredded Monterey Jack cheese, if desired.

Makes 8 servings
Joan Winnon

TONIA'S TURNIP GREENS AND BEAN SOUP

1 16-oz pkg turnips greens or collard greens or mustard greens

6 c chicken broth

1 small onion, chopped

1 clove garlic, chopped

| 1 pkg Knorr dry vegetable soup | 1 16-oz can great northern beans, undrained |
| 1 pkg smoked sausage (turkey or beef) | 1 can Ro-Tel tomatoes, drained (optional) |

Slice sausage as you like. In a Dutch oven, sauté onion, garlic, and sausage in a little olive oil until softened. Add broth, beans, soup mix, Ro-Tel, and greens. Simmer about 45 minutes. Serve with cornbread.

8 servings
Joan Winnon

CREAMY WILD RICE AND MUSHROOM SOUP IN A JAR

1 2.75-oz pkg Pioneer Country Gravy Mix	1/4 c uncooked wild rice
1 tbsp chicken bouillon granules	1 c uncooked white rice
2 tbsp dried celery flakes	2 tbsp coarsely chopped dried mushrooms
1 tbsp dried parsley flakes	

Pour gravy mix into wide-mouth pint jar. In small bowl, stir together bouillon granules, onion, celery and parsley. Pour into jar to make second layer. Add layers of wild rice, white rice, white rice and mushrooms. (You can find dried mushrooms in the produce section of your grocery store.) Seal with lid. Attach gift tag (below) and decorate jar as desired.

GIFT TAG
Make this smooth and satisfying soup to give to your loved ones—it will help to keep your relationship warm and wonderful! Empty contents of jar into large saucepan or Dutch oven. Add 7 cups water. Heat to boiling. Reduce heat, cover and simmer for 25–30 minutes or until rice is tender, stirring occasionally. Garnish with chopped fresh parsley.

Makes 6 servings
Joan Winnon

FRUIT SALAD

1 large box instant vanilla pudding	1 15-oz can pineapple tidbits
1 pint buttermilk	2 cans mandarin oranges
8 oz Cool Whip	1 can sliced peaches
1 small can fruit cocktail	

Drain all fruit well. Mix pudding mix with buttermilk and fold in Cool Whip. Add drained fruit. Refrigerate.

Ivy Gene Winnon

FRUIT SALAD

1 can pineapple tidbits in its own juice

1 can peach pie filling

4 bananas

1 c strawberries

Mix together. Add small amount of pineapple juice and let stand about 1 hour before serving.

Mae Winnon Mardis

3-FRUIT SALAD

From Jessica's Kitchen

2 medium ripe bananas, sliced

1 c seedless grapes, halved

1 c pineapple chunks

3 tbsp honey mustard salad dressing

In a bowl, combine the fruit. Add dressing and toss to coat. Cover and refrigerate until serving. Makes 4–6 servings.

Kim Winnon AmRhein

CARAMEL HAWAIIAN SALAD

1 can unopened condensed milk

1 c pecans

1 large Cool Whip

2 c miniature marshmallows

1 #2 can drained chunk pineapple

2 sliced bananas

Boil condensed milk in pot of water for 3 hours. Be sure to keep can completely submerged. After boiling, remove from water and cool completely. After condensed milk is cooled, add Cool Whip and mix well. Add pineapple, pecans, and marshmallows. Stir in bananas gently. Chill and serve.

Jacque Winnon Burchfield

CHERRY SALAD

1 pkg wild cherry Jell-O

1 can drained crushed pineapple

$1/2$ c boiling water

$1 1/4$ c Coke

1 can black bing cherries

Dissolve Jell-O in boiling water. Cool. Add other ingredients. Pour in mold and chili till it sets.

8 servings
Jesse Winnon

CRANBERRY SALAD

2 pkg cranberry Jell-O

1 can whole cranberry sauce

1 large can crushed pineapple

1/2 c chopped pecans

1 orange, finely chopped

1 8-oz cream cheese (can be flavored kind)

1 pkg lemon Jell-O

1 pkg small marshmallows

1 apple, finely chopped

Mix 2 cups boiling water with 2 pkg cranberry Jell-O until dissolved. Add crushed pineapple that has been drained (save juice), pecans, and cranberry sauce with 1/2 cup cold water. Mix until all cranberry sauce is dissolved. Chill until soupy. Pour into long dish. Chill.

Second layer: Mix lemon Jell-O with boiling pineapple juice and enough water to make 1 cup. Add cream cheese and marshmallows until melted. Mix well. Pour over first layer. Chill. Pour 1/2 cranberry mixture into mold and chill until almost firm. Cover with second layer until firm. Add 1/2 cranberry mixture on top of cream cheese mixture.

Jamie Winnon Rawls

GRAPE SALAD

1 8-oz cream cheese, at room temp

1 8-oz container sour cream

1/2 c sugar

1 tsp vanilla

6 c seedless red grapes, washed and dried well

1 c finely chopped pecans (optional)

Mix first 4 ingredients well, add grapes (grapes must be dry or filling will not stick). Place in casserole dish, refrigerate.

Jamie Rawls

HEAVENLY SALAD

1 8-oz Cool Whip

1 14-oz condensed milk

1 can cherry pie filling

1 large can crushed pineapple

1 c chopped nuts

1 c miniature marshmallows

Mix all ingredients together. Pour into a casserole. Chill and serve.

**Jacque Winnon Burchfield
from Granny Warner**

ORCHARD SALAD

1 can cherry pie filling

1 large can crushed pineapple (drained)

1 can Eagle brand milk

1 large carton Cool Whip

pecans

mini marshmallows

Mix well and chill over night.

Ivy Gene Winnon

LIME JELL-O SALAD

2 pkg lemon Jell-O

2 pkg lime Jell-O

1 c mayonnaise

2 c hot water

1 large can crushed pineapple, with juice

1 lb small-curd cottage cheese

1 c chopped pecans

1 can Eagle Brand condensed milk

Combine dry Jell-Os with mayonnaise and mix well. Add hot water and other ingredients. Stir well. Pour into large flat bowl or in small molds. Chill until firm.

Makes quite a lot
Jacque Winnon Burchfield

RIBBON CHRISTMAS SALAD

1 pkg lime Jell-O

1 pkg strawberry Jell-O

1 pkg lemon Jell-O

1 c hot pineapple juice

1 3-oz cream cheese*

20 large marshmallows, cut in half

1/2 pint whipping cream

First layer: Dissolve lime Jell-O as directed on package. Pour into 8x12-inch dish. Place in refrigerator to congeal.

Second Layer: Mix hot pineapple juice in top of double boiler with lemon Jell-O. Dissolve Jell-O. Add cream cheese and marshmallows. Mix well. Whip whipping cream. Fold into Jell-O mixture. Pour over first layer. Congeal.

Third Layer: Dissolve strawberry Jell-O according to directions. Pour over second layer. Congeal.

*I used pineapple cream cheese and it was good.

*Or 1 small pkg of mini marshmallows

Note: Can use any combination of different colors of Jell-O to make a pretty salad, anytime.

Jamie Winnon Rawls

Avocado-Tomato Salad

4 med ripe avocados, peeled and sliced

3 small tomatoes, chopped

Newman's Own Light Balsamic Vinaigrette Dressing

Squeeze lemon or lime juice over avocados to keep them from turning dark. Mix together and stir until coated with dressing. Chill and serve.

Merri (Cissie) Winnon Rushing

Beet, Apple, and Cheddar Salad

8 pink and/or gold medium-sized beets

1 tbsp olive oil

1 tbsp kosher salt

1 oz extra-shard white cheddar, crumbled

1/3 Sierra Beauty or Braeburn apple, thinly sliced

20 parsley leaves, sliced length-wise

For the vinaigrette

2 tbsp grapeseed oil or grape-seed-olive-oil blend

4 tsp hazelnuts, toasted and chopped

1/2 tsp salt

1 tsp sugar

2 tbsp apple-cider vinegar

2 tsp diced shallots

Combine vinaigrette ingredients. Set aside.

Wash beets well, dry, and toss in olive oil and kosher salt. Place beets in a baking pan or dish; add 1/4-inch water. Cover pan tightly with tinfoil and cook for 40 minutes at 400°F, or until beets are easily pierced with a knife. Uncover and allow to cool before peeling by rubbing off skin.

Chop beets, then combine with cheddar and apple. Dress with the vinaigrette and toss well. Garnish with parsley and serve.

John Atkins

Broccoli Salad

2 bunches of broccoli

1/2 red onion, chopped

1 small pkg roasted and salted sunflower seed

6–8 baby carrots, sliced

1 can water chestnuts

1 c mayonnaise

2 tbsp sugar

2 tbsp vinegar

Wash, drain and cut broccoli into bite-size pieces. Then mix all ingredients and let stand overnight in refrigerator. Recipe can be adjusted to one's taste.

Serves 6–8
Joyce Atkins Keller

BROCCOLI SALAD

1 large bunch broccoli	1/2 c celery, chopped
1 large bunch cauliflower (optional)	1 c green olives, chopped
1 medium red onion, diced small	1/2 pound bacon, fried and crumbled
1 c raisins	3–4 green onions, chopped
1 can water chestnuts, chopped	1 c cheddar cheese, diced

Separate in broccoli and cauliflower into small flowerets. Mix well. Top with dressing. I put bacon in salad before serving.

DRESSING

1 c Kraft Real Mayo	2 tbsp vinegar
1/3 c sugar	

Mix well with salad. Refrigerate overnight or at least 5–6 hours.

Jamie Rawls

CAULIFLOWER-BROCCOLI TOSS

1 large head cauliflower	1 1.4-oz package dry buttermilk salad dressing
1 bunch fresh broccoli	2 tbsp sugar
1 bunch green onions, chopped	2 tbsp vinegar
1/2 c salad dressing	

Remove outer green leaves of cauliflower and break into flowerets; wash thoroughly. Set aside. Trim large leaves off broccoli; remove stalks (save stalks for use in other dishes) separate into flowerets and wash thoroughly. Combine vegetables. Toss gently. Combine remaining ingredients; mix well and pour over vegetables. Toss gently. Cover and chill overnight.

Marilyn S Winnon (Buddy)

FRESH VEGETABLE SALAD

2 medium zucchini, sliced
1 medium yellow squash, sliced
1 c fresh broccoli flowerets
1/2 c green onions, sliced
3/4 c grated Parmesan cheese

1 c mushrooms, sliced
12 oz spaghetti, broken in half
1/2 c butter
1/2 c whipped cream

Arrange vegetables on rack and place over boiling water. Cover and steam 5–7 minutes. Add mushrooms.

Cook spaghetti and drain.

Add butter, cheese and cream. Salt and pepper to taste. Toss gently. Will keep in refrigerator for several days.

Jamie Winnon Rawls

LAYERED GREEN SALAD

1/2 medium shredded head of lettuce
1/2 c grated carrots

1 c chopped broccoli
1 can drained LeSeuer Peas*
1 c sour cream

1 c mayonnaise

1 pkg buttermilk style salad dressing mix, dry
1 c grated cheese
cooked bacon, crumbled
boiled eggs

* You can use almost any vegetable you like.

Layer in order given. Combine sour cream, mayonnaise, and dry dressing. Mix well. Cover greens. Cover tightly with Saran Wrap for 8–10 hours. When ready to serve, top with grated cheese, cooked bacon and boiled eggs.

Jamie Winnon Rawls

MAE'S MAXIMS

"Defeat is not bitter unless you swallow it."

LAYERED SALAD SUPREME

1 c small macaroni, cooked

1 tbsp olive oil, to coat macaroni

3 c lettuce

1/2 c green onions

1 can green peas, drained

1 c sandwich ham, thinly julienne sliced

3 boiled eggs, sliced

Layer lettuce, onions, macaroni, green peas, ham, eggs in glass bowl. Cover with dressing.

DRESSING FOR SALAD

1 c mayonnaise

1/4 c sour cream

1 package Buttermilk dressing, dry

1/2 c cheddar cheese, grated

3 slices cooked bacon, crumbled

sliced green olives

Mix well. Cover salad and seal edges well. Refrigerate overnight. When ready to serve, top with grated cheddar cheese, crumbled cooked bacon and sliced green olives.

Jamie Winnon Rawls

SEVEN-LAYERED SALAD

1 head lettuce, torn

1 c diced celery

1/2 c chopped green pepper

6 sliced hard-boiled eggs

1 large chopped purple onion

1 can English peas (drained)

2 c mayonnaise

1 tbsp sugar

8 oz grated cheddar cheese

4 slices bacon (cooked)

Layer first 6 ingredients. Mix mayonnaise, sugar and spread over first mixture sealing around edges. Add grated cheese and crumbled bacon on top.

Vicki Mardis

CORN SALAD

2 12-oz cans Shoe Peg corn, drained

2 chopped tomatoes

1 bell pepper

1 purple onion

1 cucumber

1/2 c sour cream

4 tbsp mayonnaise

2 tbsp white vinegar

1/2 tsp celery seed

1/2 tsp dry mustard

1/2 tsp black pepper

2 tsp salt

Mix all vegetables together. Combine other ingredients and pour over vegetables. Cover and refrigerate overnight.

Mae Winnon Mardis

MEXICAN SALAD

1 head lettuce, cut to bite-size pieces

2 tomatoes, chopped

1 large onion, chopped

1–2 cans drained chili beans

semi-crushed original Fritos, to taste

shredded cheese, to taste

Catalina or Western dressing, to taste

Mix lettuce, tomatoes, onion, beans, and cheese. Just before serving, mix the Fritos and dressing. Enjoy!

Mae Winnon Mardis

MEXICAN CORN SALAD

2 cans Mexican Corn, drained

1 can sweet white & yellow corn, drained

1 c mayonnaise

1 c sour cream

2 green onions, chopped

1 small can green chilies

12 oz cheddar cheese, small cubes

Mix well, sprinkle with chili powder, and chill at least 2 hours before serving.

Jamie Winnon Rawls

TACO SALAD

1 lb ground beef

1 lb sharp cheddar cheese

1 large head lettuce

1 large onion, chopped

2 large tomatoes, chopped

1 pkg Doritos

1 bottle Catalina salad dressing

Brown meat and drain, then add grated cheese, onions, tomatoes and lettuce that has been torn apart. Add chips and dressing just before serving and toss gently.

Vicki Mardis

SPINACH-ORANGE SALAD

1/2 c sliced almonds

2 1/2 tbsp white sugar

1 11-oz can mandarin
oranges, drained

2 pkg fresh spinach, washed,
dried and chilled

1 bunch of green
onions, chopped

Place almonds and sugar in small skillet. Stir over medium heat, watching closely and stirring constantly until almonds are golden brown. Remove to small bowl; cool. Place spinach in large container. Add green onions and oranges. At serving time, add dressing and almonds; toss lightly.

DRESSING

1/4 c vegetable oil

1 tbsp white sugar

2 tbsp white vinegar

1 tbsp snipped parsley

1/2 tsp salt

1/4 tsp black pepper

dash of Tabasco sauce

Combine dressing ingredients; cover, shake well, and refrigerate.

Donna Winnon Cox

PASTA SALAD

1/2 bottle McCormick's Salad
Supreme Seasoning

1 4-oz can sliced black olives

4–8 chopped green onions

1 finely chopped tomato

1 8-oz bottle Italian dressing

1 pkg angel hair pasta

Cook pasta according to package directions. Drain. Pour in bowl. Add other ingredients. Refrigerate overnight, stirring occasionally to marinate vegetables.

Merri (Cissie) Winnon Rushing

CHICKEN SALAD

1 chicken, boiled and
deboned

sweet pickle relish (I use sweet
pickles that I can)

2 boiled eggs, chopped

salt

pepper

lots of Miracle Whip
salad dressing

1/2 jar pimento for color
(optional)

Combine all Ingredients.

Jamie Winnon Rawls

BAKED CHICKEN SALAD PIE

3 c chicken, cooked & diced

1 8-oz can sliced water chestnuts, chopped

1/2 c slivered almonds

1/2 c chopped celery

2 tbsp chopped bell pepper

2 tbsp chopped onion

1 can cream of chicken soup

1/2 c mayonnaise (I use Hellman's in cooked recipes)

1/2 c sour cream

1 tsp celery salt

1 1/2 c cheddar cheese (divided—put 1/2 c in chicken mix)

1 9-in pie crust

Mix all together, except 1 cup cheese and pie crust. Spoon into pie crust. Bake at 375°F for 30 minutes or until bubbly. Top with balance of cheese. Bake 10 minutes more. Cool 15 minutes before cutting.

Jamie Rawls

HAM SALAD FOR SANDWICHES

When I bake a ham, I mince the leftover ham in my food processor and put it in Ziploc bags and freeze. It only takes an hour or so to thaw for mixing with the following.

2 c minced ham

1/2 c sweet pickle relish

1 tbsp mustard

3 boiled eggs, chopped fine

1/2 c Kraft Real Mayo (or until desired consistency)

Mix well. Taste will differ with glaze on ham. Make sandwiches or put on lettuce for salad.

Jamie Rawls

HAM SALAD SNOWBALL

4 c ground baked ham

4 tbsp mayonnaise, or more

4 tbsp chopped sweet pickles

1 tbsp chopped onion

1 tsp Worcestershire sauce

1 tsp prepared mustard

1 tsp chili powder (optional)

1/2 c chopped peanuts (optional)

2 3-oz pkg cream cheese

2 or 3 tbsp cream

Using coarse blade, grind enough cold, baked ham to make 4 cups. Add pickles, onion and peanuts. Put mayonnaise on top of all—then mustard, Worcestershire and chili powder in mayonnaise—for easier mixing. Blend all together, adding more mayonnaise if needed. Chill several hours. Form into a ball and frost (just like a cake) with cream cheese which has been whipped until fluffy with a little of the cream. Keep both parts stiff enough so they will keep their shape in a warm dining room. Serve as a dip or spread.

Jamie Winnon Rawls

SHRIMP SALAD

1/3 c mayonnaise	1/4 c sour cream
1/4 sugar	1 tbsp chili sauce
2 tbsp lemon juice	2 c fresh boiled shrimp
2 boiled eggs	1 c diced celery
1 tbsp pimento	1 tbsp green pepper, chopped

Chill all vegetables. Combine all ingredients well. Serve on lettuce leaf.

Jamie Winnon Rawls

LEHIGH VALLEY SHRIMP MOLD

1 can tomato soup	1 medium onion, diced
1 8-oz pkg cream cheese	salt and pepper
2 env unflavored gelatin, dissolved in small amount of water	dash of Tabasco
2 pounds shrimp, cooked, peeled, deveined and diced	1 c mayonnaise
1 c diced celery	2 tbsp horseradish, drained

Heat soup and add cream cheese. Stir until cheese is melted—the mixture will be lumpy. Add dissolved gelatin. Stir in the remaining ingredients. Pour into a well-greased mold. This recipe will fill a quart mold with a small amount left over. Refrigerate until mold is set. Unmold by running a sharp knife around the edge of the mould and invert on large platter. This is a nice party salad. At Christmas it could be molded into a star, tree, or ring and decorated with leaves.

Jamie Winnon Rawls

MAE'S MAXIMS

"Three kinds of people: Those who make things happen, those who watch things happen, and those who wonder what the heck just happened."

RICE BOX SALAD

1 pound fresh shrimp, cooked, peeled and deveined

1 c cooked rice, chilled

1 8-oz can mandarin oranges, drained

12 pitted ripe olives, sliced

12 cherry tomatoes, halved

3 green onions, minced

3 cans water chestnuts, thinly sliced

1 cucumber, peeled and sliced

1 tsp salt

1/4 tsp pepper or red pepper

2 c mayonnaise

1/2 c commercial sour cream

1 hard-cooked egg yolk, mashed

juice of 1 lemon

Combine first 10 ingredients in a large salad bowl. Combine remaining ingredients in a medium bowl, stirring well to mix. Stir mayonnaise mixture into shrimp mixture, coating all ingredients well. Chill before serving.

Yield: 6 servings.
Jamie Winnon Rawls

WHITE POTATO SALAD

1 1-oz pkg ranch dressing mix

2 c mayonnaise

5 lbs unpeeled red potatoes

3/4 c chopped green onion

1 lb bacon slices

Bring a large pot of lightly salted water to a boil. Add whole potatoes and cook until tender. Drain. Run under cold water to cool and chop into 1-inch cubes. Transfer to large serving bowl and refrigerate until completely chilled.

I separate bowl, stir together ranch dressing mix, mayonnaise, and green onions. Cover and refrigerate for about 2 hours to blend flavors.

Cook bacon until crisp and allow to cool.

Stir mayonnaise mixture into potatoes. Crumble bacon into bowl and stir to distribute.

Jeff Winnon

SALAD DRESSING

1 1/2 c mayonnaise

1/3 c sugar

1/4 c ketchup

1/2 tsp pepper

1/4 tsp salt

sweet pickle juice

Mix all together except pickle juice, until sugar is melted and not grainy. Add enough sweet pickle juice to thin, about 1 tablespoon. Will keep several weeks in refrigerator.

Jamie Winnon Rawls

BLUE CHEESE SALAD DRESSING

2 oz crumbled bleu cheese	2 tsp apple cider vinegar
1/2 c mayonnaise	2 tbsp milk or heavy cream, or enough for dressing consistency
1/2 c sour cream	1/2 tsp salt and pepper

Mix well; refrigerate. Better if sets.

Jamie Winnon Rawls

DRESSING FOR COLESLAW

1 c sugar	pinch of celery salt or celery seed
1 tsp salt	1 c mayonnaise
1 tsp dry mustard	1/4 c white vinegar
1 tsp grated onion	1 bag coleslaw mix

Combine seasonings with mayonnaise and white vinegar. Mix well. Pour over coleslaw mix.

8 servings
Joan Winnon

GREEK SALAD DRESSING

1 c olive oil	1/8 c ketchup
1/2 c sugar	salt
1/4 c white wine vinegar	pepper

Mix all ingredients well and chill before serving on salad of choice.

Joyce Atkins Keller

MAE'S MAXIMS

*"You make a living by what you get,
but a life by what you give."*

BARBECUE SAUCE

2 c sugar

2 tbsp black pepper

2 tbsp chili powder

1 tbsp red pepper

1/3 c salt

9 oz tomato purée

9 oz French's mustard (measure in purée can)

Mix dry ingredients thoroughly. Add puree and mustard to dry ingredients. Put in 1/2-gallon container. Add enough vinegar to make about 1/2 gallon or to your satisfaction. Shake well.

Jacque Winnon Burchfield

CREAM SAUCE WITH CHEESE

2 cloves garlic, minced

3 tbsp butter

1/2 c chicken broth or vegetable broth

1/4 c sour cream

1/4 c whipping cream

1/4 tsp salt

1/2 tsp pepper

1 c grated Parmesan cheese

In a saucepan, sauté garlic in butter for 2 minutes. Gradually stir in broth and reduce heat.

In a bowl, combine sour cream and whipping cream, salt and pepper. Stir cheese into broth mixture. Heat thoroughly, but do not boil. Serve over pasta or meat. Top with additional Parmesan cheese, if desired.

Joyce Atkins Keller

MARINADE

3/4 c vegetable oil

6 tbsp soy sauce

1/4 c red wine vinegar

3 tbsp lemon juice

2 tbsp Worcestershire sauce

1 tbsp dry mustard

1 tbsp salt

2 tbsp black pepper

Marinade: deer: 1.2 hours; duck: 2 hours; chicken: 2 hours; duck: 2 hours.

Ivy Gene Winnon

BEEF JERKY MARINADE

2–3 lbs beef cut in 1/8-inch strips

1/4 c wine vinegar

1/2 c Worcestershire sauce

1/2 c soy sauce

2 tbsp lemon juice

2 tbsp brown sugar

1 tbsp prepared mustard

2 tbsp liquid smoke

Trim beef of all fat and cut in strips. Mix sugar, Worcestershire sauce and mustard until smooth. Add all other ingredients. Simmer until well mixed (about 1 hour). Pour over beef and marinate for about 4–5 hours at least. Layer on dehydrator trays. Do not crowd meat.

Dry 24 to 36 hours, turning and rotating trays every 12 hours. Store in Zip-loc bags. (Jason likes this to take hunting.)

Jamie Winnon Rawls

CHEESE SAUCE FOR VEGETABLES

1/2 slick oleo, melted	1 c milk
4 tsp flour	1/2 c Velveeta cheese

Cook oleo and flour until it forms a soft ball, not brown. Add milk and cook until a soup-like consistency. Add Velveeta cheese.

Lillian Winnon Atkins

JEZEBEL SAUCE

1 jar pineapple preserves	1 jar dry mustard
1 jar apple jelly	salt & pepper to taste
1 bottle horseradish	red or green food coloring (optional)

Mix all ingredients in electric mixer. This is particularly good with ham. It will keep indefinitely in refrigeration. Can be served over cream cheese with crackers.

Mae Winnon Mardis

PESTO

2 c fresh basil	1 clove garlic, minced
1/2 c Parmesan cheese, grated	3 tbsp pine nuts, toasted
1/2 c virgin olive oil	salt & pepper, to taste

Mix all ingredients in food processor until well blended. Serve over pasta, or as a spread for sandwiches or crackers.

John Atkins

PIQUANTE SAUCE

4 qts ripe tomatoes	2 c cider vinegar
4 onions	6 tsp salt
4 cloves garlic	4 tsp sugar
4 bell peppers	1 tsp cumin
8 or 10 jalapeño peppers	1 tsp oregano

Grind and mix good first 5 ingredients. Add cider vinegar, salt, sugar, cumin and oregano. Simmer uncovered on low for an hour or until desired consistency. Put in jar and seal.

Jamie Winnon Rawls

SEAFOOD SAUCE

1 c ketchup
2 tbsp horseradish

2 tbsp Worcestershire sauce
2 tbsp lemon juice

Mix well. Any of this can be altered to taste. It is better after it sets awhile.

Jamie Winnon Rawls

RED SEAFOOD SAUCE

1 bottle ketchup
juice of 2 lemons
hot sauce to taste

Worcestershire sauce to taste
horseradish to taste

Mix well and let set a while before serving.

Jamie Winnon Rawls

TARTAR SAUCE

2 c mayonnaise

4 tbsp dill pickles, finely chopped
1 tsp chili sauce (optional)

1 bunch green onions, finely chopped
1 jar capers, finely chopped

Mix well. Let set for a while before serving.

Jamie Winnon Rawls

SEASONING SALT

26-oz box salt
2-oz bottle red pepper
1-oz bottle chili powder

1 1/2 oz ground black pepper
1-oz bottle ground garlic
1-oz Accent or MSG

FOR SEAFOOD ADD:

1 tsp powdered thyme
1 tsp sweet basil

1 crushed bay leaf

Thoroughly combine all ingredients.

Lillian Winnon Atkins

MEATS & MAIN DISHES

Poultry

KING RANCH CASSEROLE

1 5–6-lb chicken, stewed, boned and cut into bite-sized pieces

1 package corn tortillas cut in fourths

1 medium onion

1 c grated cheddar cheese

1 can cream of mushroom soup

1 can cream of chicken soup

1/2 c chicken broth, reserved from stewed chicken

1/2 c Ro-Tel tomatoes with chilies

Preheat oven to 350°F. Spray a casserole dish with cooking oil and make layers starting with the diced chicken, tortillas, onions and cheddar cheese (reserve a bit of the cheese to sprinkle on top of the casserole toward the end of cooking). In a sauce pan, heat up the soups, chicken broth, and tomatoes with chilies. Pour over the layered ingredients in the casserole. Bake for 1 hour.

Kim Winnon AmRhein

LIGHT KING RANCH CHICKEN CASSEROLE

1 large onion, chopped

1 large bell pepper, chopped

Pam

2 c chicken breasts, cooked and chopped

1 can cream of chicken soup, undiluted

1 can cream of mushroom soup, undiluted

1 can diced tomatoes and green chilies

1 tsp chili powder

1/2 tsp pepper

1/4 tsp garlic powder

12 6-in corn tortillas

1 8-oz cheddar cheese, shredded (or 3-cheese bag)

Sauté onion and bell pepper in a large skillet coated with cooking spray over medium high heat 5 minutes until tender. Stir in chicken and next six ingredients. Remove from heat.

Tear tortillas into 1-inch pieces. Layer half of the tortilla pieces in bottom of a 9x13-inch casserole dish coated with Pam.

Top with the half chicken mixture and half cheese. Repeat layers.

Bake at 350°F until cheese is melted and bubbly.

Joan Winnon

CHICKEN CASSEROLE

1 pkg seasoned bread stuffing	1/2 c chopped onion
1 stick melted butter	1/2 c chopped green onion
1 c water	1/2 c chopped celery
2 1/2 c diced chicken	1/2 c mayonnaise

Mix together seasoned bread stuffing, melted butter, and water. Mix diced chicken, chopped onion, chopped green onion, chopped celery, and mayonnaise. Put over bread mix in casserole. Top with remaining bread mixture.

Topping

2 eggs slightly beaten	3/4 tsp salt
1 1/2 c milk	

Pour over casserole, cover with, and refrigerate overnight. To bake: spread one can cream of mushroom soup over top. Bake uncovered 40 minutes in at 350°F. Remove and sprinkle with grated cheese.

Kim Winnon AmRhein

CHICKEN CASSEROLE

1 chicken or 6 chicken breasts, boiled	1 c sour cream
1 can each cream of chicken soup, cream of mushroom soup	1 1/2 c Ritz or Townhouse crackers, crumbled
1/4 c melted margarine	

Mix cracker crumbs and margarine. Put half of mixture in bottom of flat casserole dish. Mix soups and sour cream (I sometimes use 2 tablespoons of red cooking wine) and cup of chicken. Pour mixture over crumbs and top with remaining crumbs. Bake 325°F for 30–35 minutes.

Jamie Winnon Rawls

CHICKEN-BROCCOLI CASSEROLE

4 chicken breasts

1 2-oz bag broccoli

1 1/2 c rice

1 8-oz jar jalapeño Cheez Whiz

black pepper to taste

1 jar mild Cheez Whiz

1 can cream of chicken soup

1 can cream of mushroom soup

1 soup can milk

Boil and debone seasoned chicken breast. Cook broccoli. Season to taste. Cook rice in chicken broth. Heat soup, Cheez Whiz, and milk. In a 9x13-inch or larger dish, layer broccoli on bottom. Add 1/2 of soup mixture to rice. Add black pepper. Pour over broccoli. Arrange chicken on top, then pour remaining soup mixture on chicken. Heat in oven until bubbly.

Mae Winnon Mardis

CHICKEN POT PIE

1 chicken, boiled and deboned

1 stick butter

2 tsp baking powder

1 can milk

2 c chicken broth

1 can cream of chicken soup

1 can Veg-All vegetables

1 c plain flour

1 tsp salt and pepper

Place a layer of chicken in casserole dish. Pour 1 can of Veg-All on top, with juice. Melt butter and pour over this. Mix flour, baking powder, salt, pepper, and milk. Pour over mixture in dish. Mix broth and cream of chicken soup. Pour on top of entire mixture. Bake at 350°F for 45 minutes.

Ivy Gene Hamby Winnon

CHICKEN POT PIE

1 chicken, cooked and diced

1/2 small can green peas

1/2 c chopped onion

1/2 c chopped celery

2 carrots, chopped

2 c broth

1/2 c flour

Drain peas. Coat peas and diced chicken. Cook celery, carrots, and onions in broth until tender. Add milk to this. Pour broth mixture over chicken and peas. Put in large casserole dish. Top with favorite biscuits and bake 350°F until biscuits are brown. Approximately 45 minutes.

Jamie Winnon Rawls

CHICKEN POT PIE

1 chicken cooked and deboned

2 cans cream of chicken soup

1 can cream of celery soup

$1/2$ c chicken broth

1 16-oz can Veg-All, well drained

black pepper, to taste (no salt)

5 boiled eggs

Mix all ingredients except chicken and eggs in a large bowl. Put about half of mixture in a large pan or baking dish. Add chicken and sliced boiled eggs. Then add the other half of mixture. Top with crust.

Pie Crust

1 c self-rising flour

1 c milk

$3/4$ c mayonnaise

Mix and pour over chicken mixture. Bake at 350°F about 45 minutes or until brown.

Joan Winnon

CHICKEN AND LEEK PIE

From the Tea and Sympathy restaurant in NYC.

1$1/2$ lbs chicken breasts

1 large carrot, peeled and chopped

1 stalk celery chopped

$1/2$ onion, chopped

2 bay leaves

6 whole peppercorns

2 sticks butter, divided

$3/4$ c flour (use a tad more if needed)

1$1/4$ c milk

1$1/4$ c heavy cream

$1/2$ tsp of salt and same of pepper

3–4 leeks, trimmed and thinly sliced (I used 3)*

1 store-bought pie crust

1 egg, slightly beaten

*If you haven't used leeks before, you need to rinse thoroughly after the slicing because they can have a lot of dirt in them.

Put chicken in large saucepan. Cover with water to 2 inches over the chicken. Bring to a boil and then simmer for 30–35 minutes. Remove veggies from the broth, saving 2$1/2$ cups of the broth. Toss the veggies. Chop the chicken and place it in a deep pie dish. Melt $3/4$ cup butter in a saucepan. Add flour and cook about 2 minutes, then add the broth, stir, add the milk and heavy cream and stir. It took me about 20 minutes before the sauce thickened to a medium-thick gravy-type sauce. I would stir and then let it cook, etc. Add salt and pepper to taste.

In a skillet, melt a stick plus 2 tablespoons of butter and sauté the leeks until nice and soft. Add to the chicken in the pie dish. Pour the sauce over the chicken and leeks and stir to combine. Place the pie crust over the mixture. Slit top of pie crust 3 times. Brush the top with the slightly beaten egg. Preheat oven to 350°F and cook for about 45 minutes or till the crust is golden brown.

Kimberly Winnon AmRhein

CHICKEN & SPAGHETTI

1 box spaghetti	1 jar pimentos
1 large chicken	3 cans cream of mushroom soup
1 large onion (chopped)	1 large block Velveeta cheese
1 stalk celery (chopped)	1 can chopped mushrooms
1/4 c butter	milk

Boil and debone chicken and chop. Sauté onions, bell pepper, and celery in butter. Mix all ingredients together in large casserole dish. Add milk until you can stir mixture. Cook in 350°F oven until bubbly.

Ivy Gene Winnon

BABO'S CHICKEN SPAGHETTI

Good Recipe from Gail Winnon.

1 package chicken breasts, boiled in water	3 tbsp Crisco shortening
12 oz package of spaghetti	2 tbsp flour
1 or 2 bell peppers	1 onion
1 can tomato paste	1 c chopped celery
1 can Ro-Tel tomatoes	dash of red pepper
1 clove of garlic	1 tbsp chili powder
salt and pepper to taste	

Sauté bell pepper, garlic, onion and celery in shortening and flour mixture. Add tomato paste, Ro-Tel tomatoes, red pepper, and chili powder. Simmer a few minutes. Add all of this to cooked spaghetti that has been drained. Cut up chicken and add to mixture. You may use the broth from cooking breasts for more moisture. Cook 15–30 minutes after all ingredients have been combined.

Joan Winnon

CHEESY CHICKEN AND SPAGHETTI

1 whole chicken or 4 chicken breasts

1 onion

2 stalks celery

1 bell pepper

1 can Ro-Tel tomatoes

1 can cream of chicken soup

1 pkg spaghetti

Velveeta cheese

Boil chicken with plenty of water so you can have enough broth. Add to this onions, celery and bell pepper cut in large pieces. Boil until chicken is tender. Remove, let cool, then debone. Strain broth, removing the 3 other ingredients (this is done because most kids don't want to eat them, but you still get the flavor). To the broth add Ro-Tel tomatoes and cream of chicken soup, and boil until soup is dissolved. Add spaghetti, cook until almost done, then add cheese (as much as you want). Let melt. Be sure the heat is low. Then add chicken mixture. Turn off heat and cover.

READY TO EAT WHEN YOU ARE!

Mae Winnon Mardis

AUNT VERA'S CHICKEN SPAGHETTI

1 fryer

1 can stewed tomatoes

1 large can tomato paste

1 chopped onion

1 pkg spaghetti

1 chopped bell pepper

3 tbsp Worcestershire sauce

3 tbsp chili powder

4 bay leaves

Boil fryer and let cool. Salt and pepper to taste. Mix above ingredients into broth from chicken, about 3 quarts needed. Add deboned chicken and let cook for 15 minutes. Add uncooked spaghetti. Let simmer until spaghetti is done.

Donna Winnon Cox

MAE'S MAXIMS

" Sin will take you further than
   you want to go,
Keep you longer than you want to
   stay,
And cost you more than you want
   to pay."

CHICKEN MARSALA TETRAZZINI

1 8-oz package vermicelli

2 tbsp butter

1 8-oz package sliced
fresh mushrooms

3 oz finely chopped
prosciutto ham

3 c chopped
cooked chicken

1 c frozen baby English peas,
thawed

1 10 3/4-oz can reduced-fat
cream of mushroom soup

1 1-oz container refrigerated
light Alfredo sauce

1/3 c chicken broth

1/4 c Marsala sauce
(I use chicken broth)

1 c (4 oz) shredded
Parmesan cheese

Preheat the oven to 350°F.

Prepare pasta according to package directions. Meanwhile melt butter in a large skillet over medium-high heat. Add mushrooms and prosciutto and sauté for 5 minutes.

Stir together mushroom mixture, chicken, next 5 ingredients, and 1/2 cup of cheese. Stir in pasta.

Spoon mixture into a lightly greased 11x7-inch baking dish. Sprinkle with remaining 1/2 cup of cheese.

Bake 35 minutes or until bubbly!

Remove pasta mixture from the heat. Stir in sour cream. Serve with chicken.

> Note: This recipe was prepared with Lipton Pasta Sides fettuccini in a chicken-flavored sauce mix.

8 servings
Joan Winnon

SOUTHERN CHICKEN PATTIES

I made these often when my children were home.

1/3 c butter

1/2 c flour

2 1/4 c milk

2 c chopped, cooked chicken

1/2 c crushed Premium Crackers
(Saltines)

2 tbsp chopped parsley

cooking oil

1/2 tsp onion salt

dash pepper

1 egg

1 c finely rolled Premium
Cracker crumbs

1 tbsp water

1/2 lb Velveeta, sliced

Make a cream sauce with the butter, flour, and 1³/₄ cup milk. Combine chicken, ¹/₂ cup Premium cracker crumbs, parsley, seasonings, egg, and 1 cup of the sauce. Chill. Shape into 8 patties. Roll in crumbs. Fry in hot oil (375°F) until golden brown. Blend ¹/₂ cup milk with remaining sauce; heat. Add Velveeta and stir until melted. Spoon over patties.

Makes 8 patties
Terri Winnon

EASY CARIBBEAN JERK CHICKEN

This has great flavor and my kids LOVE it when I make this!

1 env Italian salad dressing mix	1 tsp cinnamon
2 tbsp brown sugar	1 tsp thyme
2 tbsp oil	¹/₂ tsp ground red pepper
2 tbsp soy sauce	2 ¹/₂ lbs chicken pieces

Mix all ingredients (except chicken) in a bowl. Pour over chicken. Marinate AT LEAST 1 hour (overnight is better) in the fridge. Put on hot grill and grill until juices run clear.

Kimberly Winnon AmRhein

CHICKEN MEXICAN DISH

2 5-oz cans boneless chicken	8-oz jar of Cheez Whiz
2 cans chicken soup	2 tbsp chopped onion
1 c chicken broth	3 chili peppers
2 tsp pimento (chopped)	1 tbsp chili powder
1 large pkg Doritos	

Mix all ingredients, except Doritos in saucepan. Simmer 15 minutes. Crush Doritos and place half Doritos in bottom of baking dish. Pour in mix, then cover with remaining Doritos. Bake 25–30 minutes at 375°F.

FAJITA CHICKEN

3–4 boneless, skinless chicken breasts	1 tbsp Fajita seasoning
olive oil	salt
pepper	

Brown chicken breast in olive oil. Add seasoning and cook on low heat until chicken is done. Drain. Serve with garlic pasta.

Garlic Pasta

1 pkg linguini (thin)
4–6 chopped green onions
1–2 cloves garlic (pressed)

2–4 tbsp margarine
1–2 tbsp olive oil
salt

Cook linguini. Drain. Set aside. Sauté onions and garlic in olive oil until onions are tender. Add butter. Stir in pasta and stir until well coated and mixed. Add salt. Heat until warm. Serve pasta with fajita chicken. Add salad and bread for complete meal.

Merri (Cissie) Winnon Rushing

Chicken Burritos

3 chicken breasts, boiled and deboned
1 pkg 10 flour tortilla
1 bunch green onions, chopped
2 tbsp pimento
1 tbsp fajita seasoning

1 can cream chicken soup

1 c sour cream
1 c Monterey Jack cheese (grated)

1 c cheddar cheese (grated)

Sauté onions, pimento, and chicken. Add fajita seasoning. Mix soup and sour cream together. Assemble burritos by placing chicken mixture on each tortilla. Spoon soup mix over chicken mixture. Sprinkle with cheese. Roll each burrito and place in baking dish. Spread remaining cheese on top. Bake at 350°F for 20–30 minutes, until hot. Serve with salsa if desired.

*Best if covered with plastic wrap and cooked in microwave on high for 10 minutes or until cheese is melted.

Merri (Cissie) Winnon Rushing

Chicken Enchiladas

6 chicken breast halves with bone
1 can condensed cream of chicken soup
1 8-oz carton sour cream
1 small pkg Velveeta Mexican cheese

1 small chopped onion

1 pkg flour tortillas

2 c Monterey Jack cheese

Cook chicken and cut into bite-size pieces. Soften tortillas. Sauté onion in small amount margarine; mix in soup, sour cream and Velveeta until cheese is melted. Set 1/4 of sauce aside for topping; add chicken to remaining sauce. Put small amount of mixture into tortilla; roll up and place seam-side down in 13x9-inch baking dish.

Pour reserved sauce over top of filled tortillas. Sprinkle Monterey Jack cheese over top; bake at 350°F for 15 minutes or until cheese is melted and casserole is bubbly.

**Melinda Mardis Bryan,
daughter of Mae Winnon Mardis**

CREAMY CHICKEN ENCHILADAS

1 tbsp butter or margarine

1 medium onion, drained

1 can chopped green chilies, drained

1 8-oz pkg cream cheese (I use jalapeño flavored)

1/2 tsp salt

1/2 tsp pepper

2 c whipping cream

1/2 tsp chili powder

3–4 c cooked chicken, chopped

8 8-in tortillas, softened on a grill

1 8-oz pkg Monterey Jack cheese, shredded

1 8-oz pkg Monterey Jack/ Colby cheese shredded

1 can Cream of Chicken soup

Sauté onion until clear. Add green chilies, cream cheese, salt, pepper, chili powder, and cooked chicken. Stir well. Spoon 2–3 tablespoons chicken mixture onto each tortilla and a small amount of shredded cheese. Roll tightly. Lay in flat casserole dish, seam down. Mix cream of chicken soup with whipping cream. Sprinkle remaining cheese on enchiladas and pour cream of chicken mixture over cheese. Bake at 350°F for 45 minutes.

Jamie Winnon Rawls

DUMPLINGS

From Mamaw Beatrice Hamby

1 1/2 c self-rising flour

3 tbsp Crisco

3/4 c milk

Cut Crisco into flour, until pea sized. Add milk and stir. Roll out thinly and cut into strips, or drop by teaspoonfuls into hot chicken broth, or Mamaw would take a can of Cream of Chicken soup and add water to desired amount of liquid. DO NOT STIR, just move dumplings around with spoon. Cover. Cook over low heat for 15–20 minutes. Remove cover and stir. Mamaw used to make these for Rachel a lot. Tastes wonderful even without the chicken. Of course I use the same recipe for the dumplings when I used a cooked, deboned fryer added to it. Season to taste.

Donna Winnon Cox

CHICKEN AND DUMPLINGS

1 medium onion chopped

2–3 boneless skinless chicken breast (boiled and cut up)

1 can cream of chicken soup

2 tbsp instant bouillon (chicken)

salt and pepper

2 tbsp butter

2 c flour

milk

water

Sauté onions in 2 tbsp butter until tender. Add 2 cups water and chicken soup. Add chicken and bouillon, and 1 tbsp salt and pepper. Add 1 more cup water and 1 cup milk. Cook over medium heat. Mix flour in bowl with 1 tsp salt and 1 tbsp bouillon. Gradually add mixture of half milk and half water until thick ball forms. Roll flour mixture out on floured board approximately 1/4-inch thick. Cut slices (pieces about 3 inches long, 1 inch wide). Let dry for about 10 minutes. Slowly add pieces to liquid mixture, stirring while adding. Let cook over low heat until done, stirring occasionally to prevent sticking.

Merri (Cissie) Winnon Rushing

CHICKEN AND DUMPLINGS

1 fat fryer

1 1/2 tsp salt

3/4 tsp black pepper

3 c plain flour

shortening (enough to resemble a large egg)

1 egg (optional)

1 heaping tsp salt

1 tsp baking powder

Cover fryer with a lot of water. Add salt and black pepper. Boil until ready to fall off the bones. You will need to add some water from time to time. Take meat off the bones and discard skin, fat, and bones. Reserve the broth.

DUMPLINGS

Cut all ingredients together with a pastry blender. Add cold water a little at a time until a large ball of dough forms. Divide the dough into four small balls. I like to make my dough the night before and place in a bowl covered with foil in refrigerator. Sprinkle dough board with flour. Roll one piece at a time. Sprinkle with flour and cut into small pieces. Drop into boiling broth and cook about 15 minutes or until done when tested. Add chicken and bring back to a boil. If there is not enough broth add some canned broth. You will want to have plenty of broth.

Barbara Foster Oliver

Mrs. Bobbie's Chicken and Dumplings

1 hen cooked with salt and pepper, deboned

1 1/2 c self-rising flour

1 small can Carnation milk

1/2 stick butter

Moisten flour with warm tap water. Roll thinly, cut into strips (about 3x1 1/2 inches). Add dumplings one at a time in hot boiling broth with chicken. Add carnation milk and butter. Turn stove off as soon as you get the dumplings in broth. Let set about 45 minutes to 1 hour before serving.

Jamie Winnon Rawls

New Orleans Dumplings

BROTH

2 cans cream of chicken soup

2 cans golden mushroom soup

2 tbsp minced onion

2 1/2 c water

1/2 c chopped green pepper

DUMPLINGS

2 c cooked, chopped chicken

1/4 c celery

2 tbsp minced onions

1 tsp parsley flakes

2 tsp pepper

1 can buttermilk biscuits (10)

In a large saucepan, combine soups, water, green pepper, and minced onion. Heat, stirring occasionally until bubbly. Combine all ingredients for dumplings, except biscuits, in a large bowl. Roll out each biscuit into a 4-inch circle. Place approximately 1/4 cup chicken mixture on each circle. Fold dough over mixture and press edges together. Place sealed edges of dumplings down in bubbly soup mixture; cover and cook on medium heat for 20–30 minutes. Serves 6.

Jacque Winnon Burchfield

Ritz Cracker Chicken Breast

4–6 chicken breasts

melted butter

seasoning salt

Ritz crackers, crushed

Remove skin from chicken. Sprinkle with seasoning salt. Dip chicken in melted butter and roll in crushed Ritz crackers. Bake at 350°F 45 minutes.

Melinda Mardis Bryan

CREAMY BAKED CHICKEN BREASTS

From Mom and Aunt Clara.

4 chicken breasts, deboned, cut in half

8 slices of Swiss cheese

1 can cream of chicken or mushroom soup

1/4 c dry white wine, optional

1 c herb seasoned stuffing mix

1/4 c melted margarine

Arrange chicken in a lightly greased (Pam) 13x9-inch baking dish. Top with cheese slices. Combine soup and wine, or use chicken broth). Stir well. Pour over chicken just before you put chicken in oven. Sprinkle the stuffing crumbs on top. Pour melted margarine on crumbs.

Bake at 350°F for 45–50 minutes. You can add cooked minute or regular rice to the casserole.

Joan Winnon

ITALIAN STUFFED CHICKEN BREASTS

6 boneless, skinless chicken breasts, thawed

salt

pepper

1 c soft bread crumbs

1/2 c shredded smoked mozzarella cheese

1/4 c chopped pepperoni

2 tbsp olive oil

1/2 c water

With a sharp knife, carefully slit a pocket in meaty part of each breast. Season breasts with salt and pepper. In small bowl, combine bread crumbs, cheese, pepperoni and pepper. Stuff filling into breasts; fasten closed with toothpicks. In a large frying pan, heat olive oil over medium-high heat. Add breasts and cook, turning once, 3–5 minutes, or until browned on both sides. Add water and bring to a boil. Reduce heat to low, cover and cook 20–30 minutes, or until tender and white throughout, turning once. Remove toothpicks and serve with warm marinara sauce.

Serves 6
Joyce Atkins Keller

CHICKEN BREAST PARMESAN

4 boneless, skinless chicken breasts

1/4 c Parmesan cheese

1/2 tsp oregano

1 can cream of chicken soup

1/2 c milk

4 slices Swiss cheese

bread or cracker crumbs

Dip chicken in mixture of Parmesan and oregano. Put in casserole. Cover with cheese. In sauce pan, combine soup and milk; warm to remove lumps. Pour over chicken. Top with crumbs and any remaining Parmesan. Bake at 350°F 30–35 minutes.

Jamie Winnon Rawls

SOUTHERN FRIED CHICKEN

1 cut-up chicken (I use chicken breast)	salt
garlic salt	pepper
buttermilk	self-rising flour

Salt chicken with garlic salt. Cover with buttermilk and let set for at least 1 hour. (Sometimes I leave it overnight.) Mix self-rising flour, salt, and pepper. Drain chicken and roll in flour mixture. Heat oil in heavy skillet. Cook chicken on medium heat until almost done. Turn heat up to brown crispy.

Jamie Winnon Rawls

DIVINE CHICKEN DIVAN

6–8 chicken breasts, cooked and deboned	2 c mayonnaise
1 c shredded American cheese	1 tbsp lemon juice
4 pkg frozen chopped broccoli	1 tsp curry powder
3 cans cream of chicken soup	1 1/2 c toasted bread crumbs
1/4 c milk	1/2 c pimiento strips (optional)

Cook broccoli as directed on package. Drain. Arrange in a buttered 9x13x2-inch Pyrex dish. Place chicken on top. Combine soup, milk, mayonnaise, lemon juice and curry powder. Pour over chicken. Sprinkle with cheese. Top with bread crumbs. Bake at 350°F for 25–30 minutes. Garnish with pimiento strips if desired.

Marilyn S Winnon (Buddy)

MAE'S MAXIMS

"If we did all the things we are capable of, we would literally astound ourselves."

GUMBO

4 tbsp oil	1 can chicken breast (or 2 cooked chicken breasts cut up)
1/4 c flour	1 lb Cajun sausage (cut up)
1 medium onion, chopped	1 lb peeled deveined shrimp
4–6 chopped green onions	Creole seasoning
1 can diced tomatoes	salt
1 small can crab meat	pepper
1–3 tbsp gumbo filé (to taste)	

Sauté onions in 2 tbsp oil until tender. Add shrimp and sausage. Cook until shrimp are done. Set aside. Brown flour in 2 tbsp oil until dark brown. Gradually add water, stirring to keep smooth. Add water until thin. Add tomatoes, shrimp, onions, sausage, crabmeat, and chicken. Stirring occasionally, continue to simmer for about 30 minutes. Add more water if needed. Slowly add filé a small amount at a time, being careful to avoid clumping. Gumbo will thicken some with the addition of the filé.

Merri (Cissie) Winnon Rushing

TEAM ROPING GUMBO

1 chicken	Tony's Creole seasoning
1 onion	6–8 eggs
1 lb link sausage	gumbo filé

Boil chicken with chopped onion and a little black pepper. Debone and remove skin from chicken. Skim off any oil or fat. Put chicken and sausage both in broth. Heat oil in skillet. Stir in flour for thickness desired. Cover with Tony's and stir. Cover with filé and stir. Brown and stir into gumbo. Stir well. Bring to a boil (may add water). Turn down heat. Crack and carefully drop eggs in gumbo. Let eggs cook, then carefully stir gumbo. Serve over rice.

Keith Myers

CHICKEN AND SAUSAGE GUMBO

3/4 c oil	salt and pepper to taste
3/4 c flour	1 tsp thyme
1 onion chopped	2 quarts of chicken broth or 4 cans
1 stalk celery, chopped	1 pound smoked sausage, sliced

1 16-oz can tomatoes
(can be stewed tomatoes)

3 tbsp creole seasoning
(I use Tony Chachere or any
good seasoning)

5 chicken breasts cut in bite
size pieces

Make roux: Heat oil in heavy pot, add flour, and brown on medium heat until roux is the color of a penny. This takes about 15–20 minutes. Stir constantly or roux will burn. If it burns, start over. Add: onion and celery and sauté until onions are clear. Add tomatoes, creole seasoning, salt and pepper to taste, thyme, and chicken broth. Cook over low heat for 30 minutes. Brown smoked sausage, sliced, and 5 chicken breasts. Add browned meat to sauce. Cook 30 minutes on low heat. Stir often to prevent sticking and scorching. Serve over rice. Add a sprinkle of gumbo filé to each serving.

Variation: Use any seafood instead of chicken or sausage.

Jamie Winnon Rawls

Roux

equal parts cooking oil and flour

Heat oil in heavy iron pot until hot, then gradually add flour while stirring constantly. After combining the flour, lower the fire and continue to stir constantly until copper-colored. May be used in gumbo or most creole recipes.

Lillian Winnon Atkins

Cajun Chicken

1 fryer

butter or oil for browning

$2/3$ c flour

$3/4$ c butter

2 onions, chopped

3 bell peppers, chopped

1 c hot water

1 bay leaf

2 tsp Worcestershire sauce

3 dashes hot sauce

1 12-oz can mushrooms

Salt and pepper chicken. Brown lightly in butter or oil. Make a roux of flour and butter. Add chopped vegetables to roux and stir until slightly soft. Slowly add hot water, stirring constantly. Add chicken and seasonings. Cover and simmer about 1 hour. Stir occasionally to prevent sticking. Add mushrooms the last 10 minutes. Serve over rice.

Jacque Winnon Burchfield

Cajun Étouffée

1/2 lb link sausage, sliced

2 chicken breasts boiled and deboned

1 small pkg imitation crabmeat

1 stick butter

2 Tbsp flour

2–4 c hot water

2 chopped onions

1 bell pepper (cut up)

1 stalk celery (cut up)

1/2 c green onion tops (chopped)

cooked rice

Tony's Creole Seasoning

cayenne pepper

salt and pepper

Sauté onions, peppers, and celery in butter until tender. Add flour, then meat, and stir until well blended. Add water to desired consistency. Season with cayenne pepper, salt, and black pepper to taste. (A little Tony's Creole Seasoning is good also.) Add onion tops and simmer until tender. Serve over cooked rice.

Merri (Cissie) Winnon Purvis

Chicken Spectacular

3 c cooked chicken

1 can cream of celery soup

1 medium jar sliced pimento

1 medium onion, chopped

salt and pepper to taste

2 c French-style beans, drained

1 pkg Uncle Ben's combination white and wild rice, cooked as directed on package

1 c Hellmann's mayonnaise

1 can water chestnuts, drained and sliced

Mix all ingredients. Cook in 2 1/2-quart casserole dish at 350°F for 25–30 minutes. Do not cook before freezing. Let thaw completely to cook.

Serves 16
**Joan Winnon &
Jamie Winnon Rawls**

Chicken Rolls

3 or 4 boiled chicken breasts, cut fine

1 onion, chopped fine

8 oz shredded cheddar cheese

1 jar spicy pimentos

1 can chicken broth

dash of celery seed

1 can cream of chicken soup

1 can cream of celery soup

1 can evaporated milk

Roll chicken breasts, onion, cheddar cheese, pimentos, and celery seed into 24 small balls—approximately 1 tablespoon each. Place in wide part of crescent roll, bring corners up and long end around and enclose mixture. Place in deep 9x13-inch pan. Mix soups well and pour over chicken rolls. Bake uncovered at 350°F until brown.

Jacque Winnon Burchfield

MOROCCAN TAGINE

Authentic Moroccan dish from Mahmoud Assadek.

1 whole chicken, cut into pieces	2 bay leaves
1/2 c olive oil	1/2 tsp thyme
1 eggplant, cut in large cubes	1/2 tsp oregano
4 potatoes, cut in large cubes	salt and pepper
1 c green and red pepper, chopped	1 tbsp Adobo seasoning
4–5 carrots, sliced	2 chicken bouillon cubes
2 large onions, chopped	1 large can tomato sauce
4 stalks celery, chopped	1 can tomato paste
6 c water	

COUSCOUS

1 box couscous	1/4 c raisins
2 tbsp butter	1/4 sliced almonds

Wash chicken and sauté in 1/4 cup of oil for 5–8 minutes over medium heat in a Dutch oven or tagine. Add tomato sauce and 2 cups water and bouillon cubes. Cook for another 15 minutes. Add thyme, oregano, bay leaves, Adobo, salt and pepper. Add 2 more cups of water. Add all chopped vegetables, raw, and can of tomato paste. Cook another 30 minutes on medium heat. Add more water as needed to keep a liquid consistency. Cook couscous according to package, with 2 tsp butter. When fully cooked, stir in almonds and raisins and fluff with fork.

Variation with Lamb

Season 1 leg of lamb with herbs and spices. In Dutch oven or tagine, pour in 2 cups water and 2 beef bouillon cubes (omit tomato sauce and tomato paste.). Cook at 350°F for 1 1/2 hours, until meat is done. Add water as needed to prevent meat from drying. Add raw vegetables about 1 hour into cooking time. Serve with couscous, prepared as above.

John Atkins

BUFFALO WINGS

A real favorite!

3 lb chicken wings

1 stick butter

4–8 tbsp hot sauce

bleu cheese dressing (Marie's)

Cut up wings. Deep fry till golden brown and crisp. Drain. In saucepan melt butter and add hot sauce to your liking. Pour into large plastic container. Add wings, seal tightly, and shake. Let stand in refrigerator a couple of hours. Serve with Marie's Blue cheese dressing, carrot and celery sticks. The longer they stay in fridge the hotter they get.

Gail Winnon Williams

CORNISH HENS

4 Cornish hens

1 tsp tarragon

4 cloves garlic

salt

Sprinkle each hen with tarragon, 1 clove garlic and salt. Let stand in refrigerator covered 8 hours. Bake in shallow pan at 400°F for 1 hour, basting every 15 minutes.

BASTING SAUCE

1 1/2 c margarine

2 tbsp tarragon

1 1/2 c dry white wine

I have also done these on the grill. Same way, basting every 15 minutes (excellent). I have also used this recipe with pheasant.

Gail Winnon Williams

FRIED TURKEY

2 c Italian dressing

2 c A-1 steak sauce

2 c Worcestershire sauce

5 oz Tabasco sauce

cayenne pepper to taste

5 oz soy sauce

3 tbsp onion salt

3 tbsp garlic salt

3 tbsp seasoned salt

Combine all ingredients; inject into turkey. Mix 2 tbsp Tony's and 2 tbsp mustard. Rub over turkey. Place in plastic bag overnight to marinate. Using 3–5 gallons of peanut oil—maintain a temperature of 350°F. Fry 5 minutes per pound rotating so that it cooks evenly.

Mae Winnon Mardis

Smoked Turkey

1 8–12 lb turkey

1 large bag Pepperidge Farm stuffing

1/2 cup, celery, green pepper, green onions, chopped fine

Sauté vegetables. Prepare stuffing and add sautéed vegetables. Mix well. Stuff turkey.

Basting Sauce

1 c butter with 2–3 dashes of the following:

garlic powder

hot sauce

thyme

cinnamon

poultry seasoning

red pepper

onion powder

salt

celery salt

pepper

In medium saucepan heat ingredients. Prepare coals around a drip pan placed in center of grill (in direct heat). When coals are hot, place turkey on grill with foil folded to about 4x8 inches underneath. Cover and grill 15–25 minutes, then baste every 15–20 minutes till done—about 3–4 hours depending on size. I have found when turkey is done, close vents and let sit for 30 minutes–1 hour, then remove and slice and serve.

Gail Winnon Williams

Smoked Turkey Roll

1 8-oz pkg cream cheese

2 c smoked turkey, chopped

3 tbsp mayonnaise

1 c pecans, chopped

Put cream cheese, mayo, and turkey in food processor or chopper. Mix until well blended. Form rolls. Roll until coated in pecans. Refrigerate until ready to serve.

Merri (Cissie) Winnon Rushing

Thanksgiving Leftover Breakfast Bake

Left-over turkey and dressing

Toppings (such as crumbled bacon, cooked sausage, chopped onions, chopped peppers, chopped mushrooms)

12 eggs, scrambled

grated American cheese

Grease casserole pan and spread dressing on it. Pour eggs over dressing. Sprinkle with left-over turkey and other toppings. Bake at 350°F for 30 minutes. Sprinkle cheese on top and bake an additional 10 minutes. Cut into squares and serve.

Joyce Atkins Keller

Beef, Pork, etc.

SUNDAY ROAST BEEF

1 rump roast	1 onion, sliced
salt and pepper	1 c hot water
3 tbsp hot oil	2 tbsp flour

Salt and pepper roast on all sides. Brown in hot oil until all sides are brown. Sauté onion until clear. Stir in 2 tbsp flour and 1 cup hot water. Cover with tight lid. Cook 350°F for 30 minutes, then turn heat to 250°F. I cook this until I get out of church. If I add potatoes, I add them before I leave for church. Everything is ready when I get home. This is a good hint to use on all cooked meats: Slice across the grain for best tenderness.

Jamie Winnon Rawls

BAR-B-QUE BRISKET

1–4 to 10 lb trimmed brisket	garlic salt
1 tbsp liquid smoke	celery salt
onion salt	1 bottle Italian salad dressing

Sprinkle brisket with liquid smoke. Then sprinkle with onion salt, garlic salt, and celery salt. Rub into meat good. Cover with Italian salad dressing. Cover tightly with foil and refrigerate overnight. Add enough water to almost cover meat and bake 3 to 4 hours at 300°F or until tender. Scrape off fat. Put on grill for 1 hour. Turn often. Add bar-b-que sauce if desired. Cool. Slice. Tastes like you smoked all night.

Jamie Winnon Rawls

PEPPER STEAK

2 pounds chuck steak, cut into strips	2 large green peppers, cut into strips
2 tbsp minced onion	2 tbsp cornstarch
1 clove garlic, minced	2 tsp water
1/2 celery sliced	1 tsp soy sauce
1 can consommé	

Brown meat in shortening. Slowly add onion, garlic, celery, and green peppers. Add consommé. Season with salt and pepper. Simmer, covered 20 minutes. Thicken with cornstarch blended with water and soy sauce. Simmer for 5 minutes. Serve hot with rice or Chinese noodles. Serves 4. Sometimes I add 2 quartered tomatoes 5 minutes before end of cooking time.

Jamie Winnon Rawls

ROUND STEAK CASSEROLE

2 lb round steak
(cut in strips)

garlic salt, salt, and pepper beans

1 onion, sliced thin

3–4 potatoes, quartered

1 16-oz can French-style green beans

4 cans tomato sauce

1/2 c water

Season steak with salt and pepper. Place in bottom of pot. Place sliced onion on steak. Add potatoes and green beans. Top with tomato sauce and water. Cover and bake 350°F for 3 hours.

Jacque Winnon Burchfield

SLICED BEEF AND SPAGHETTI

1 1/2 lb of trimmed round steak, sliced as thin as possible

1 small onion, chopped

1 small bell pepper, chopped

1 10-oz can diced tomatoes and chilies

1 6-oz can tomato paste

3 oz sweet and sour sauce

1 tbsp Worcestershire sauce

1 tbsp onion powder

1 tsp garlic powder

5 large mushrooms, diced

1 c Parmesan cheese

16 oz spaghetti, cooked

1 tbsp butter

1 tbsp canola oil

In a large Dutch oven, melt butter and add oil. Heat on medium high and add steak. Brown thoroughly and add water and cook until meat is tender, adding water as needed. Add diced tomatoes and chilies, tomato paste, Worcestershire sauce, onion powder, garlic powder, and water if needed. Do not add so much water that your sauce becomes too thin. Simmer for another 20 minutes. Add mushrooms and cook an additional five minutes. Add sweet-and-sour sauce and let stand for 5 minutes. Serve over cooked spaghetti and sprinkle with Parmesan cheese.

Jacque Winnon Burchfield

BARBECUED ARM ROAST

This has been a favorite of mine for years (especially in the lean ones) when I wanted something really good for little money for guests. It has never failed me. Back in the old days we would cover it with a roasting pan lid. Now with covered grills!

3 lb roast (1 1/2–2 inches thick)	1 tbsp Worcester sauce
1/3 c red wine vinegar	1 tsp prepared mustard
1/4 c catsup	1 tsp salt
2 tbsp cooking oil	1/4 tsp pepper
2 tbsp soy sauce	1/4 tsp garlic powder

Combine red wine vinegar and next eight ingredients. Mix well. Place roast in large roasting dish or large plastic bag. Pour marinade over roast and refrigerate at least 4 hours (overnight is fine) turning 2 or 3 times. Cook roast on grill covered about 1 hour, turning and basting with marinade every 15 minutes (less time for rare).

Gail Winnon Williams

CHUCK ROAST BARBECUE

1 2–2 1/2 lb boneless chuck roast	1 tsp beef bouillon, granular
2 medium onions, chopped	1/2 tsp dry mustard
3/4 c cola	1/2 tsp chili powder
1/2 c Worcestershire sauce	1/4 tsp ground red pepper (cayenne)
1 tbsp apple cider vinegar	1/2 c catsup
2 cloves garlic, minced	2 tbsp margarine

Combine roast and onion in 4-quart crock pot. Combine cola and all other ingredients. Pour over roast and cook covered on high 6–7 hours till tender. Slice or shred.

I did this with a venison roast. Cooking it on the stove in a Dutch oven till done with onions. Then shredded meat and cooked in sauce till well blended. Served on hamburger buns. It was great.

Gail Winnon Williams

BEEF AND PEPPER RICE SKILLET

1 round steak cut in thin strips	1 can consommé soup
2 tbsp cooking oil	1 soup can water
1 c sliced onion	2 green peppers, chopped
1 c rice	

Brown beef in oil. Stir in onion, rice, soup and water. Bring to boil. Reduce heat, cover and cook over low heat until liquid is absorbed—

about 20 minutes. Stir in green peppers, cover, and remove from heat.

Mae Winnon Mardis

Big Pot of Stew

When Lillian and my kids were small we made stew quite often and each time tried to perfect it in some way.

stew meat (I like to use deer steak cut into pieces—they are always tender)	2–3 c water
1 large onion, chopped	carrots
cooking oil	1 can chopped, seasoned tomatoes
flour, seasoned with salt and pepper to taste	potatoes, cut into pieces

Sauté onions in pot. Roll meat lightly in seasoned flour and brown with the onions. The flour makes the liquid slightly thicker. Add water when meat is brown. Add as many carrots as you like, can of tomatoes, and potatoes. If the liquid gets too thick you can gradually add water to your own.

Mae Winnon Mardis

FOOD FUNNIES

❋ from Mae Winnon Mardis

This is my all-time stew story: Melinda was a baby and I had just come home with her. My sister-in-laws Ivy Gene and Terri came over to make us a pot of stew—in the pressure cooker. All went well until they were taking the top off and didn't let all the steam out first. You can guess, it blew up, and meat, potatoes, and carrots were stuck on the ceiling. I can't remember if there was enough to eat or not!

TEXAS MEATBALL STEW

1 lb ground beef
1 egg, beaten
1/2 c dry bread crumbs
2 tbsp milk
1 c water

1/2 tsp salt
1 can tomatoes
1 c elbow macaroni
1 pkg chili mix

Combine ground beef, egg, bread crumbs, milk and salt. Mix well and shape into 1-inch balls. Brown on all sides and drain. Add tomatoes, beans, uncooked macaroni, chili mix and water. Bring to boil stirring gently to avoid breaking meatballs. Reduce heat and simmer for 15 minutes.

Mae Winnon Mardis

CHILI SEASONING MIX

3 tbsp flour
2 tbsp minced onion
1 1/2 tsp chili powder
1/2 tsp ground cumin

1/2 tsp crushed red pepper
1 tsp salt
1/2 tsp minced garlic
1/2 tsp sugar

This can be mixed as needed for your chili. The following recipes can be used with this mix: Ranch-Style Chili; Texas Meatball Stew; Beef and Pepper Rice Skillet; Beef Taco Casserole. Use this mix as chili mix.

Mae Winnon Mardis
& Brenda Winnon Myers

RANCH STYLE CHILI

1 lb ground beef

1 pkg chili mix

1 small can tomato sauce, rinsed with water
1 can chopped tomatoes

Brown ground beef in large skillet and drain. Stir in chili mix, tomato sauce and tomatoes. Bring to boil, reduce heat and simmer covered about 10 minutes.

Mae Winnon Mardis

DIRTY RICE

This will feed many, many people. This is the dish Barry always brings to our family gatherings.

1 lb ground meat

1 lb smoked sausage

1 lb pork

2 c rice

1 can golden mushroom soup

1 can French onion soup

1 can cream of mushroom soup

1 medium can mushrooms

2 bundles green onions, chopped

1 bell pepper, chopped

1/2 onion, chopped

Brown meat and set aside. Sauté chopped onions and bell peppers. Cook rice. When done, add all soups and mushrooms in a large pot. Add the meat last and bake 30 minutes at 300°F.

Teresa Mardis (Barry's wife)

PORCUPINE MEATBALLS

1 lb ground beef

1/2 c uncooked rice

1/2 c chopped onion

1 tbsp Worcestershire sauce

1 tsp salt

1 can tomato sauce

1 1/2 c water

Combine meat, rice, onions, and salt. Mix well. Form into balls. Place in baking dish. Combine tomato sauce, water, and Worcestershire sauce. Pour over meatballs. Cover dish and bake for 1 hour in 350°F oven.

Donna Winnon Cox

MAE'S MAXIMS

" I am only one, but I am one. I cannot do anything, but I can do something—and what I should do and can do, by the grace of God, I will do."

MEXICAN QUICHE

1 lb ground beef

1/2 onion, chopped

1 bell pepper, diced

1 can cream style corn

1/2 lb grated sharp
cheddar cheese

1 pkg Mexican cornbread mix

1 tbsp oil

Brown meat with onions and bell pepper. Mix cornbread mix according to package directions. Add a little more than half the can of corn to cornbread mixture. Heat oil in skillet. Pour in half the cornbread mixture. Place meat mixture on top of batter. Sprinkle cheese on top of meat mixture. Add remaining corn, then rest of cornbread. Spread to cover top. Bake in 400°F oven until cornbread is done. Cool slightly. Serve in wedges.

Serves 4 to 6
Donna Winnon Cox

ENCHILADAS

1 1/2 lbs hamburger

2 cans enchilada sauce

1 pkg flour tortillas

1 can cream of mushroom
soup

2 c shredded cheese

Brown hamburger meat. Drain. Add cream of mushroom soup and 1 can of enchilada sauce. Mix well. Fill tortillas with mixture, roll up, and place seam side down in baking dish, lightly sprayed with Pam. Any meat left over can be poured on top of tortillas. Layer cheese on top and pour other can of enchilada sauce over that. Bake at 350°F for 30–35 minutes.

Brenda Winnon Myers

ENCHILADA CASSEROLE

1 lb lean ground beef

1 large onion

2 c salsa

1 15-oz can black beans, rinsed
and drained

1/4 c reduced fat Italian salad
dressing

2 tbsp reduced-sodium taco
seasoning

1/2 c fresh cilantro, minced

1/4 tsp ground cumin

6 8-in flour tortillas

3/4 c reduced-fat sour cream

1 c (40 oz) shredded reduced-
fat Mexican cheese blend

1 c lettuce, shredded

1 medium tomato, chopped

In a large skillet, cook beef and onion over medium heat until meat is no longer pink. Drain.

Stir in the salsa, beans, dressing, taco seasoning, and cumin. Place 3 tortillas in a 2-quart baking dish coated with cooking spray. Layer with half of the meat mixture, sour cream, and cheese. Repeat layers. Cover and bake at 400°F for 25 minutes. Uncover, bake 5–10 minutes longer or until heated through. Let stand for 5 minutes before topping with lettuce, tomato, and cilantro.

8 servings
Joan Winnon

SANCHILADAS

1 lb ground beef	10 flour tortillas (large)
1 tbsp cumin	1 large can red enchilada sauce, mild
1 tbsp chili powder	2 small cans green enchilada sauce, mild
1/2 c chopped onions	sour cream
2 c Mexican blend cheese	1/2 tsp garlic

Combine ground beef, cumin, chili powder, onions, and garlic in skillet. Sauté until beef and onions are done. Drain. Set aside. Place 1 tbsp sour cream about 1 inch from one edge of flour tortilla. Top sour cream with 2 tbsp meat mixture. Sprinkle with cheese. Roll up tortilla and place seam down in baking dish sprayed with cooking spray. Continue method until all tortillas are filled. Mix enchilada sauces together. Pour over tortillas, making sure sauce goes between each one. Cover with remaining cheese. Bake at 350°F until cheese is melted and sauce is bubbling (20–30 minutes), or cover with plastic wrap and cook in microwave for 10 minutes. Microwave method works best and is quicker.

Merri (Cissie) Winnon Rushing

TEXAS-STYLE LASAGNA

1 1/2 lb ground beef	1 can green chilies, chopped
1 tsp seasoning salt	1 medium cottage cheese
1 pkg taco seasoning mix	2 eggs, beaten
1 can Mexican diced tomatoes, drained	12 corn or flour tortillas, torn
1 can tomato sauce	1 bag of shredded Monterey Jack cheese

Mix the cottage cheese and eggs together.

Brown ground meat and drain. Add seasoning salt, taco seasoning, tomatoes, tomato sauce, and chilies. Mix well. Simmer uncovered for 15–20 minutes.

In a greased 13x9-inch pan, layer half of meat sauce, half of the tortillas, half of the cottage cheese mixture, and half of the cheese. Repeat layers. Bake uncovered at 350°F for 30–40 minutes. Let stand about 10 minutes.

8 servings
Joan Winnon

Hot Tamales

corn shucks	1/2 c cornmeal
2 lb hamburger meat	1/2 c water
2 med onions, chopped fine	1 c tomato sauce
2 pods garlic, chopped fine	3 tbsp chili powder
2 tbsp salt	1 or 2 tsp cumin
2 tsp red pepper	

Mix all ingredients together. Boil corn shucks for a few minutes.

Cornmeal Mixture

2 c cornmeal	1 tsp red pepper
2 1/2 tsp salt	

Put 1/2 tsp cornmeal mixture on wet corn shuck. Then add a small amount of meat mixture on cornmeal. Then add 1/2 tsp cornmeal mixture on top of meat. Roll corn shuck tightly and pack tightly in heavy cooking pot.

Sauce

1 small can tomato paste	1 tsp salt
2 tbsp chili powder	

Mix all well and pour over tamales. Add water to cover tamales 1/2 inch. Cook for 1 1/2 hours. Start on medium heat to get boiling then lower heat to a slow boil and cover.

Mae Winnon Mardis

*" Beware of getting into a panic—
it's bad for the natural heart and
destructive to the spiritual life."*

MEXICAN STACK-UPS

cooked rice

homemade chili

corn chips

chopped lettuce

chopped peanuts

chopped tomatoes

chopped onion

cheese sauce
(made with Ro-Tel tomatoes)

chopped ripe olives

salsa

Make cheese sauce with Velveeta cheese and Ro-Tel tomatoes, melted together in double boiler or microwave.

The amount of each of these ingredients depends on how many you plan to feed. These are good for any large group of people. Stack ingredients as you wish with rice on bottom and topped with cheese sauce. Remember to start out with a large plate, because it seems to grow.

Mae Winnon Mardis & Joan Winnon

TACOS

1 lb ground beef, browned

1 pkg taco seasoning

1 c water

onions

taco sauce in jar

tomatoes

cheese

taco shells

shredded lettuce

Combine ground beef, taco seasoning, and water and cook until thick. Spoon meat mixture into taco shells and top with other ingredients.

Lillian Winnon Atkins

TACO SEASONING

2 tbsp chili powder

small amount of salt & pepper

dash oregano & onion salt

Mix all together and use. Equivalent of 1 store-bought package.

Mae Winnon Mardis

PISTOLETTES

1 pkg. pistolette rolls

1 lb ground beef
and/or sausage

1 large jar Cheez Whiz
or Velveeta cheese

1 large onion, chopped

Tony's seasoning to taste

Take lid off rolls. Pull centers out of rolls and make into bread crumbs. Brown meat with chopped onion and seasoning. Do not drain. Add crumbs with meat and mix with cheese. Fill rolls with mixture. Melt 2 tbsp butter, add garlic powder to taste, then brush onto rolls. Bake in oven until brown.

Sometimes I use chili powder instead of Tony's and hot sausage can be used, which changes the taste altogether. Broccoli can be used in the meat mixture also.

Mae Winnon Mardis

CORN BREAD PIE

1 c corn meal

3/4 c self-rising flour

salt

black pepper

red pepper

pinch of sugar

1 c buttermilk

1/4 c water

2 eggs

cheese

1 small onion, chopped

jalapeño pepper

1 tbsp baking powder

1 8 3/4-oz can cream corn

1/4 c cooking oil

Combine all ingredients. Warm cooking oil in skillet. Pour some into mix and then mix well.

MEAT FILLING

1 lb hamburger meat

1/4 c bell pepper, chopped

1/4 c onion

3/4 c grated cheese

salt, to taste

black pepper

red pepper

jalapeño pepper

Preheat oven to 450°F. Put meat in skillet with other ingredients and brown meat. Drain excess fat. Pour about 1/2 of cornbread mixture into skillet, spread meat on top, then pour the remaining mixture on top. Bake until golden brown.

Jacque Winnon Burchfield

MEATBALLS AND SPAGHETTI SAUCE

1 to 2 lbs ground meat

1 egg, beaten

1 stale bun or 1 stale
slice of bread

2 tbsp Italian seasoning

salt and pepper to taste

olive oil

1 c chopped onion

2 cloves garlic

1 tsp chili powder

1 can tomato paste

1 can tomato sauce

1 can tomatoes

2 c water

2 tbsp brown sugar

2 tbsp Italian seasoning

1 tsp basil

1 tbsp ground oregano

Mix well first 5 ingredients and shape into balls. Fry in about 1 inch of olive oil until brown on all sides. Remove from oil. Pour off all oil except enough to sauté chopped onion. Add garlic and tomato paste to onions. Brown with onion. Add rest of ingredients. Add meatballs. Simmer at least 1 hour on low heat. (I usually add about 1/4 cup cooking burgundy wine—this adds a better flavor.)

Jamie Winnon Rawls

HAMBURGER HELPER

1 1/2 lb hamburger meat

1 can tomato soup

1 can cheddar cheese soup

1 1/2 c cooked noodles

Brown meat. Drain. Stir in soups. Cook until hot. Stir in noodles.

Brenda Winnon Myers

BRENDA'S QUICK DISH

1 lb hamburger meat

1 can Ranch Style beans

1 can Spanish rice

cheese

Brown hamburger meat. Drain. Stir in beans and rice. Pour in casserole dish and layer with cheese. Bake at 350°F until hot.

Brenda Winnon Myers

LILLIAN'S MEAT LOAF

YUM YUM GOOD!!!! This is from Bobby's cousin Lillian Holcomb Phillips and it is good.

2 lb ground chuck

3 tbsp catsup

1 envelope onion
Recipe Secrets

1 1/2 tsp sage

2 eggs

6 or 8 crackers (crushed)

TOPPING

3 tbsp catsup   3 tbsp brown sugar
3 tbsp mustard

Mix first six ingredients together well. Place in meat loaf pan and cook at 350 until done. Then mix topping and spread on top of meat and leave in oven 5 more minutes.

Mae Winnon Mardis

PIZZA MEAT LOAF

1 1/2 to 2 lbs lean ground beef   Italian spices (oregano, garlic, basil, parsley), to taste

6- or 8-oz pkg mozzarella   salt and pepper
cheese

ham, thin-sliced   1 egg

1 15-oz can Hunt's Italian
tomato sauce

Mix meat with egg, spices, and about one cupful of tomato sauce. Pat out on wax paper into a large rectangle about 1/4-inch thick. Cover with ham slices and cheese (save some cheese for top). Roll up jelly-roll style. Put seal side down. Pour on remaining tomato sauce. Bake about 45 minutes to one hour at 350°F. Last 5 minutes top with remaining cheese. Bake until cheese melts. Let sit for a few minutes before slicing. Enjoy!

June Winnon Dawkins

MAE'S MISC

How to Fringe

Cut strands of yarn 12 inches long.

Hold 3 strands for knot of fringe together.

Fold in half.

Pull folded ends of strands through edge to be fringed.

Draw loose ends through folded end.

Pull knot securely.

NATCHITOCHES MEAT PIES

FILLING

1 1/2 lb ground beef
1 1/2 lb ground pork
1 tsp–1 tbsp shortening
1 tsp coarsely ground black pepper
1 tbsp salt

1/2 tsp cayenne
1 c chopped green onions
1 pod garlic, minced
1 bell pepper, chopped

1/3 c flour

Melt shortening in heavy pot with salt, pepper, cayenne, green onions, garlic, and bell pepper. Add beef and pork and stir over medium heat until meat turns brown. Sift flour over meat. Stir well. Cool to room temperature and drain in a large colander.

CRUST

1 qt flour
1/2 tsp oregano
1/2 tsp red pepper
1/2 tsp white pepper
1/2 tsp lemon pepper
1/2 tsp dry mustard

2 tsp salt
1/2 tsp onion salt
1 tsp baking powder
1 egg
1/2 c shortening
1 c milk

Sift dry ingredients together. Cut in shortening. Beat egg and add 1 cup milk. Work gradually into dry ingredients until proper consistency to roll. Roll 1/2 at a time on floured board, very thin. Cut in 5-inch circles with a saucer for a cutter (3-inch circles for cocktail size).

Place 1 tbsp of filling on one side of circle (1 tsp for smaller size). Moisten edges, fold over meat, and crimp edges with moistened fork. Prick top twice with fork. Deep fry in oil at about 350°F until deep golden brown. Meat pies freeze well. Freeze on cookie sheets and store in plastic bags. Do not thaw before cooking.

Makes about 18
**Lillian Winnon Atkins
& Jacque Winnon Burchfield**

MEAT BUN BAKE

1 1/2 lb ground round
1/2 tsp pepper
2 c chopped cabbage
1 c shredded cheddar cheese
2 eggs

1/4 c chopped onion
1 1/2 c Pioneer Biscuit mix
1/2 tsp salt
1 c milk

In a skillet, brown meat; drain. Add cabbage, onion, salt and pepper; cook over medium heat for 15 minutes or until cabbage and onion are tender. Stir in cheese; spoon into a greased 13x9x2-inch baking dish. Blend biscuit mix, eggs, and milk. Pour over beef mixture. Bake uncovered at 400°F for 20–25 minutes or until golden brown.

Jacque Winnon Burchfield

UPSIDE-DOWN PIE

1 lb ground meat
1 tbsp shortening
1/2 c chopped onion
1/2 tsp salt
1/2 c chopped celery

1 can tomato soup
1/4 c chopped bell pepper
1 1/2 c biscuit mix
1/2 c milk
3 slices cheese

In skillet, brown beef, onion, celery, and bell pepper. Stir in salt and soup. Combine biscuit mix and milk. Spread meat mixture evenly in skillet; top with biscuit dough. Bake at 450°F for 15 minutes. Turn upside down to serve and top with cheese.

Jacque Winnon Burchfield

BREAKFAST CASSEROLE

2 cans crescent rolls
6 eggs
bacon (optional)

1 1/2 c grated cheddar cheese
1 lb pan sausage

Brown sausage and drain. Grease a 9x13-inch baking dish and line with 1 can crescent rolls. Combine eggs, cheese, and cooked sausage; pour over crescent rolls. Top with other can of crescent rolls. Bake at 325°F until golden brown.

Mae Winnon Mardis

BREAKFAST CASSEROLE

1 lb pork sausage, browned
onions, chopped
bell pepper, red, green, and yellow, chopped
celery, chopped
1 can cream of chicken soup

garlic, pressed
1 c uncooked rice
salt and pepper

1 can cream of mushroom

Mix ingredients together in a baking dish, and bake in oven, covered, 1 hour at 350°F.

Jacque Winnon Burchfield

BEAJAY'S MEAL-IN-ONE CORNBREAD

1 box cornbread mix

1 15-oz can whole kernel corn

1 15-oz can cream corn

1/2–1 lb sausage

1 med onion, finely chopped (optional)

green pepper, finely chopped (optional)

Mix cornbread as directed. Add corn, sautéed sausage, onions, and pepper. Cook at 450°F until done (about 15 minutes).

Jacque Winnon Burchfield

SAUSAGE CASSEROLE

1 lb pan sausage

1 onion, chopped

2 soup cans of water

1 tsp hot pepper, chopped

1 bell pepper, chopped

1 can cream of chicken soup

3/4 c uncooked rice

Cook sausage until done—drain if very fat. Add onions, bell pepper and hot peppers. Cook until done. Add soup and water. When mixture comes to a boil, add rice. Cook covered 10–15 minutes until rice is done to consistency of your choice.

Serves 4–5
Ivy Gene Winnon

SAUSAGE AND RICE CASSEROLE

This was always a favorite with my kids.

1 lb bulk sausage (kind optional)

1 c each chopped green onion, celery, bell pepper

1 c rice, uncooked

1 can Golden Mushroom soup

1 can cream of chicken soup

2 soup cans water

Brown sausage in pan and drain. Add chopped vegetables and simmer until tender. Add cans of water as you rinse cans. Mix all ingredients and bake for 1 1/2 hours at 350°F. Stir occasionally and add water if needed.

Mae Winnon Mardis

SAUSAGE RICE PILAF

1 lb hot pork sausage

1/2 c chopped onions

1/2 c chopped green peppers

1 c chopped celery

1 can cream of
mushroom soup

1 c dry rice, cooked separately

1 can whole kernel corn

Cook sausage over low heat in a large skillet, pouring in grease now and then, and stirring to crumble the meat. Add onion, green pepper, and celery and cook for 5 minutes. Stir in soup and cooked rice. Pour into casserole, cover, and bake at 255°F for 30 minutes.

Jesse Winnon

SAUSAGE GRAVY

1/2 lb pan sausage

1 tbsp cornstarch

1 c skim milk

salt & pepper to taste

Brown sausage in skillet. Dissolve cornstarch in milk. Add to sausage. Season with salt and pepper to taste.

Mae Winnon Mardis

JAMBALAYA

1 lb smoked sausage

2 c rice

1 lb shrimp

1 medium onion

4 c chicken broth

garlic salt

1/2 tsp thyme

salt and pepper

2 c canned tomato

Brown smoked sausage, rice, and shrimp (any kind of meat may be used). Set aside. Brown onion, garlic, thyme, and salt and pepper. Add rice and meat mixture. Add tomatoes and chicken broth. Cover and cook on low heat 1/2 hour.

Jamie Winnon Rawls

EASY PULLED PORK

3–4 pork butt roast

2 cans Ro-Tel tomatoes

black pepper

2 small cans green chilies

garlic salt

Season the roast with salt and pepper. Place roast in crockpot on high. Add all ingredients. Bring to a boil; reduce to low heat. Cook for 8 hours. Serve on buns as sandwich or over rice.

Joyce Atkins Keller

JAMIE'S HOT DOG CHILI

10 lbs ground chuck

6 oz chili blend (I use Morton)

3 oz chili powder (Mex-ann)

3 medium onions, chopped

3 8-oz cans tomato sauce

6 8-oz cans water

1 small jar garlic powder

3 tbsp brown sugar

1 small can tomato paste

1 bottle ketchup

1/2 c cracker meal (approximately)

Brown meat and onion. Drain, if lots of liquid. Add tomato paste until hot. Add all other ingredients. Simmer 1 hour. Add water and cracker meal until desired thickness. Chili can be stretched by this method also.

Jamie Winnon Rawls

PORKCHOPS AND RICE CASSEROLE

6 pork chops

1 c rice (dry)

1 c beef bouillon

salt and pepper

6 slices onion

6 slices bell pepper

1 can tomatoes

Brown pork chops, remove, and brown rice in drippings. Layer pork chops on rice. Put onion and pepper on pork chops, then pour bouillon over all of that. Top with tomatoes. Bake in 350°F over for 1 hour covered.

Jamie Winnon Rawls

PORKCHOP POTATO CASSEROLE

8 pork chops, 1/2 inch thick

1 tsp seasoned salt

1 tbsp vegetable oil

1/2 c sour cream

1/2 tsp salt

1/4 tsp pepper

cream of celery soup

26-oz frozen shredded hash browns

2/3 c milk

2.8-oz French fried onions

1 c grated cheese

Sprinkle pork chops with seasoned salt. Brown chops on both sides in oil. In a large bowl, combine soup, milk, sour cream, salt and pepper. Stir in hash browns, 3/4 c cheese, and half of onions. Spread into greased 9x13x2-inch dish. Arrange porkchops on top. Cover and bake at 350°F for 40 minutes. Uncover, sprinkle with remaining cheese and onions. Bake uncovered 5–10 minutes or until potatoes are tender, cheese is melted and meat juices run clear.

Jacque Winnon Burchfield

HASH BROWN AND PORKCHOP CASSEROLE

1 can cream of mushroom soup	1 24-oz pkg frozen hash browns, thawed
1/2 c milk	1/2 c shredded cheddar cheese
1/2 c sour cream	1 can French fried onions
1/2 tsp seasoned salt	1 tbsp oil
1/4 tsp black pepper	1/2 c shredded cheddar cheese

Combine first five ingredients in a bowl and mix well. Spoon into a sprayed 9x13-inch dish.

Brown the pork chops in hot oil. Arrange them over the potato mixture. Bake covered at 350°F for 40 minutes.

Top with remaining 1/2 cup cheese and onions. Bake uncovered for 5 minutes.

Marilyn S Winnon (Buddy)

PORKCHOPS OVER RICE

boneless porkchops	1 cube beef bouillon
1 can beef consommé soup	rice

Brown pork chops on both sides. Pour consommé soup over them. Dissolve beef bouillon cube in water (as directed on package). Pour over pork chops. Bring to boil. Turn heat down and simmer until chops are tender. Cover.

Cook rice according to directions and top with pork chops.

Morgan Watson Johnston

MAE'S MAXIMS

" Instead of complaining that the rosebush is full of thorns, be happy the thornbush has roses."

BUTTERY HAM AND CHEESE SANDWICHES

12 (1 pkg) potato or Hawaiian rolls

1/2 lb deli-shaved Black Forest ham

4–6 slices Swiss* cheese (thin sliced)

1 stick butter

1 tsp poppy seeds

1 tsp prepared mustard, honey mustard, or Durkee sauce

1 tsp Worcestershire sauce

1 tsp dehydrated onion flakes

Line a baking sheet with foil. Slice the package of rolls in half, forming a top and bottom and removing the "top" in one piece. Do not separate the rolls from one another. Layer the ham and cheese on the bottom half of the rolls. Replace the "top".

Place the butter, mustard, Worcestershire sauce, onion flakes, and poppy seeds in a small saucepan and heat until the butter is melted. Pour the butter mixture over the rolls and cover the pan with foil. Place in the refrigerator overnight.

Bake covered at 350°F for 15 minutes. Remove the foil and bake an additional 5 minutes. Cut into individual sandwiches. Hint: The sandwiches come apart "cleaner" if you allow the rolls to sit for a few minutes before trying to cut them.

*You can also add mozzarella cheese in addition to the Swiss.

**Jacque Winnon Burchfield
& Mae Winnon Mardis**

HAM AND CHEESE WITH POTATO CRUST

1 24-oz pkg frozen hash browns, thawed and drained

1/3 c butter or margarine, melted

1 c cooked ham, diced

1 c Monterey Jack cheese, shredded finely

1 c cheddar cheese, shredded finely

2 eggs, slightly beaten

1/2 c milk

1/4 tsp seasoned salt

Preheat oven to 425°F. Grease a 9-inch pie pan with shortening. Press the hash browns between a towel to remove excess moisture, then press the potatoes into and up the sides of a greased pie pan. Brush with the melted butter and bake for 20 minutes. Layer the ham and both cheeses into the baked crust. In a small bowl, combine the eggs, milk, and seasoned salt until well blended. Pour over the layers of ham and cheese. Reduce oven temperature to 350°F and bake for 35 minutes, or until a knife inserted in the center comes out clean.

Makes 8 servings
Kim Winnon AmRhein

HASH BROWN QUICHE

From Katherine Edmiston

1 24-oz pkg frozen shredded hash browns, thawed	1 c (6 oz) diced cooked ham
1/3 c melted butter	1/2 c milk
1 c (4 oz) shredded hot pepper cheese	2 eggs
1 c (4 oz) shredded Swiss cheese	1/4 tsp salt

Grease 9-inch pie plate with solid shortening or butter. Press thawed hash browns between paper towels to remove excess moisture. Fit hash browns into pie plate. Brush hash brown crust with melted butter; be sure to brush top edges. Bake at 425°F for 25 minutes. Remove from oven and fill with cheeses and ham. Beat milk, eggs, and salt; pour over cheese and ham. Bake at 350°F for 30–40 minutes.

Jacque Winnon Burchfield

SPAM CASSEROLE

1 7 1/2-oz pkg macaroni & cheese dinner	1 c chopped tomato
1 12-oz can whole kernel corn, drained	1 can Spam cut into 12 strips
1 can cream of celery soup	1 tbsp chopped parsley

Prepare dinner as directed on package. Add corn, soup, tomato, and parsley. Mix well. Layer half of dinner mixture and luncheon meat in 1 1/2-quart casserole. Repeat layers. Bake at 350°F for 25–30 minutes or until hot. Garnish with parsley, if desired.

4–6 servings
Lillian Winnon Atkins

DONNA'S ZESTY VENISON CHILI

2 lb ground venison	1/4 tsp cayenne pepper
1 large onion, chopped	1/2 tsp black pepper
1 green pepper, chopped	1/2 tsp oregano
1 8-oz can tomato sauce	1 tsp cumin
1 c water	2 cloves garlic, finely chopped
2 tbsp chili powder	1 tsp salt

Brown meat, onion, and green pepper. Drain any fat. Add remaining ingredients. I cook mine in my small pressure cooker at 15 lb for 5 minutes, but is just as good cooked in conventional cook pot. Simmer for 1 hour.

Donna Winnon Cox

TED'S FRIED DEER STEAKS

deer steaks	milk
salt water	flour
Italian Salad dressing	salt and pepper
3 eggs	

Soak steaks in salt water 2 or 3 hours. Wash, then soak in salad dressing about 2 or 3 hours. Remove and dip in flour seasoned with salt and pepper, then dip in egg and milk mixture, then again in flour. Fry in hot vegetable oil until brown. Don't overcook or the meat will be tough.

Ted Mardis

OLE FASHION POSSUM

It's best to catch a posssum and put him in a cage and feed for a couple of weeks to clean him out. He may have been eating a dead horse or cow, or anything that is dead, and you wouldn't want that. Feed him good and fatten him up—the fatter the better. This is how it was done during and after the depression.

When he gets fat lay him on his belly and put a crowbar behind his neck. Then putting your feet on the crowbar on both sides of his neck, grab his hind legs and pull up as hard as you can to break his neck. Hang him up, skin him, and get all of the musk pockets out of his neck and under his arms. The musk will make him taste bad, and you don't want that. You can then stretch his hide, and when it gets dried a fur dealer will give you around 50 cents or maybe 75. The only waste you will have is his guts and feet. You may even want to save the feet and sell them as watch fobs. You could probably sell them at a flea market for $1.50 each.

Now you are ready to cook him. Put him in a pan big enough to hold him without cutting him up. Peel and slice some sweet potatoes and place them all around, as many as you can. Add lots of salt and black pepper. Cook for at least 1 1/2 hours, or until done. This is a full meal. You not only get a good meal, but you can get some of your money back by selling his hide. Enjoy!

Jesse Winnon

Seafood

SHRIMP CASSEROLE

1 c onions (chopped)
1/4 c chopped green onions
1/2 c bell pepper (chopped)

1/2 c celery (chopped)
1 lb peeled shrimp
1/2 lb link sausage

1/4 c butter
2 c cooked rice
1 can cream of mushroom soup
1 can cheddar cheese soup
1 small jar pimento

Sauté onions, bell pepper, celery, shrimp and link sausage in butter until shrimp is done. Mix together rice, soups and pimento and add sautéed ingredients. Pour into large casserole dish and cover with foil. Bake at 350°F for 20 minutes.

Ivy Gene Winnon

SHRIMP AND SAUSAGE CREOLE

1 lb shrimp, frozen or fresh

4 oz smoked sausage, halved or sliced

1 med onion, chopped

1 med green pepper cut into bite-size pieces

1 14 1/2-oz can whole tomatoes, cut up
3 cloves garlic, minced

1 tsp Tony's seasoning (or more as desired)
2 c cooked rice

Thaw and clean shrimp, leaving tails intact if desired. Devein and rinse shrimp. Pat dry with paper towels. Set aside.

In a 4-quart Dutch oven, cook sausage, onion, and pepper over medium heat about 5 minutes until onion is tender and beginning to brown. Add undrained tomatoes, garlic, and Tony's seasoning, Stir until combined. Bring to boil; reduce heat. Simmer uncovered for 5 minutes.

Stir shrimp into sausage mixture. Return to boil; reduce heat. Cover and simmer for 2–3 minutes more or until shrimp turn pink.

Serve with rice.

8 servings
Joan Winnon

JAMIE'S SHRIMP JAMBALAYA

2 tbsp vegetable oil
2 tbsp margarine or butter
1 c sweet onion, chopped
1/2 c celery, chopped
1 c uncooked rice (long grain)
1 small can tomato sauce
1 15-oz can stewed tomatoes

2 tbsp Creole seasoning
1 tbsp fresh basil
1/4 c fresh parsley
salt and pepper to taste
1 tsp seasoned pepper
1 qt chicken broth
1 qt cooked shrimp

Melt together vegetable oil and margarine or butter. Add sweet onion and celery. Sauté until onions are clear. Add uncooked rice. Brown well. Add tomato sauce and stewed tomatoes. Get this real hot. Add creole seasoning, basil, parsley, salt and pepper, and chicken broth. Get real hot and bubbly and add cooked shrimp. Cook on low heat for 25 minutes. Stir and let sit 10 minutes.

Jamie Winnon Rawls

SAUSAGE-SHRIMP JAMBALAYA

3/4 c oil
1 lb smoked sausage, sliced 1/4-in thick
1 lb shrimp peeled and salted
2 c dry rice
1/2 c chopped celery
1 1/2 c chopped onion
1 c chopped bell pepper
2 cloves garlic

1/2 c chopped green onions
1/4 c chopped parsley

1 can stewed tomatoes
1 bay leaf
1 tsp Worcestershire sauce
1 tsp Louisiana red hot sauce
2 c water or broth
salt, pepper, and Tony Chachere's to taste

In oil, brown sausage, remove, and fry shrimp. Add rice and vegetables. Sauté until wilted. Add sausage, tomatoes, salt, pepper, and seasonings. Stir well for a few minutes. Add broth or water. Simmer for 30 to 45 minutes on low heat.

Jamie Winnon Rawls

FRIED SHRIMP

1 lb fresh shrimp, peeled
1 c flour

1 egg
3 tbsp milk

1/4 c cornmeal (yellow)

1 tbsp seafood seasoning
(I use Tony Chachere's)
over shrimp

salt, pepper to taste

Mix well flour, cornmeal, salt, and pepper. Set aside. Mix egg with milk. Sprinkle seafood seasoning over shrimp. Dip in egg mixture, roll in flour mixture, then drop in hot oil until brown. Doesn't take long.

Jamie Winnon Rawls

JAMIE'S SEAFOOD GUMBO

3/4 c vegetable oil

1 c all-purpose flour

2 large onions, chopped

4 stalks celery, chopped

1 medium bell pepper, chopped

1 16-oz can whole tomatoes, undrained or stewed

4 cloves garlic, minced

1/2 c fresh parsley, chopped

1 tsp dried thyme
(can use fresh)

2 tbsp Creole seasoning

1 tsp red pepper

1 bay leaf

4 14-oz cans chicken broth or 2 qts shrimp stock (boil shrimp shells and use drained broth)

2 or 3 lbs medium shrimp, peeled and deveined

1 lb fresh crabmeat

2 or 3 doz oysters (optional)

1 lb boiled crawfish

salt and pepper to taste

gumbo filé, to taste

Heat oil in large heavy pot. Add flour and cook over medium heat 10–15 minutes, stirring constantly until roux is the color of a copper penny. This will scorch if you do not stir often. If it burns, start over. The cooking of the roux is the secret. Stir in vegetables until onions are clear. Add chicken broth or liquid. Bring to boil. Cover, reduce heat and simmer 30 minutes, stirring occasionally. Add shrimp, crabmeat, and crawfish. Cook about 15–20 minutes longer. Add oysters and cook about 15–20 minutes longer. Add filé to individual servings unless you are going to use all of the gumbo at one time. Can be frozen if filé has not been added. Serve over rice.

RICE

2 c water, boiling

1 c rice (good long grain)

1/2 tsp white vinegar

To boiling water add rice and vinegar. Reduce heat to low. Cook 17 minutes, stir, and let set 5 minutes. Rice will be perfect and not gummy.

Jamie Winnon Rawls

SEAFOOD GUMBO

1/2 c oil	2–3 lb raw, peeled shrimp
2 1/2–3 c sliced fresh okra	1–1 1/2 lb peeled crab meat
1 tbsp vinegar	15–20 crab fingers (peeled crab claws)
1 c oil	Tony Chachere's seasoning
1 c flour	salt and pepper
1 c chopped onions	red pepper, chopped
1 c green onions	Louisiana hot sauce
1 c chopped celery	

Put oil and okra in a large pot and smother until tender. Add vinegar to stop sliminess. Roux: In a heavy skillet, heat oil. When hot, add flour; stir until brown. Add seasonings to this and simmer until onions, celery, and pepper are wilted. Season shrimp with Tony's seasoning and hot sauce. In a large stockpot, add okra, roux, and shrimp. Mix well and simmer until shrimp are pink, then add about 2 gallons of chicken broth and stir mixture into it. Cook about 1 1/2 hours on low heat. Add crabmeat and crab fingers and cook 1/2 hour more. Season to taste with Tony Chachere's seasoning, salt, pepper and hot sauce. Serve over rice.

Jacque Winnon Burchfield

SEAFOOD CREAM CHOWDER (OR BISQUE)

1 medium onion chopped	2 12-oz cans of whole kernel corn, drained (you may substitute cream style or shoe peg)
1 bunch green onions, chopped	2 8-oz pkgs cream cheese
2 cans cream of potato soup	1 qts half and half (can use fat free)
1 can cream of mushroom soup	2 pkgs crawfish tails (or shrimp or crabmeat)
1 can cream of celery soup	1 tsp Zataran's Crab Boil
1 can Ro-Tel medium or hot tomatoes, drained	1 tsp Tony Chacherie's

Sautée onions in 1/2–1 stick of butter. Add soups, tomatoes, corn, cream cheese, half and half. (If soup is too thick, you may add milk as needed.) Add crawfish. Season to taste with seasonings. (Taste before adding salt. You might not need it.) Cook over low fire at least until cream cheese melts. Stir often to prevent sticking. Enjoy!!!!

June Winnon Dawkins

SHRIMP ÉTOUFFÉE

4 lb fresh shrimp	1 tbsp cornstarch
1 stick margarine	1 tbsp tomato paste
1 c chopped onions	1 1/2 c chicken broth
1/4 c onion tops	1/2 c celery
1/2 c bell pepper, chopped fine	2 cloves garlic, pressed

Parboil and peel shrimp. Set tails aside. Mix margarine with onion, bell pepper, and garlic in heavy pot. Cook uncovered over medium heat until onions are wilted. Add shrimp tails. Let simmer, constantly, for 20 minutes. Dissolve cornstarch in chicken broth, then add tomato paste. Add to shrimp, stirring, occasionally. Season to taste with salt, black and red pepper. Bring to boil over medium heat and cook uncovered for 15 minutes. Add onion tops and parsley. Mix well. Serve over cooked rice.

**Lillian Winnon Atkins
& Jacque Winnon Burchfield**

SHRIMP ÉTOUFÉE

3 lbs shrimp, peeled and deveined	2 cloves garlic, pressed
1/2 lb (2 sticks) butter or margarine, or 6 tbsp cooking oil	1 tbsp cornstarch
2 c onion, chopped fine	1 tbsp tomato paste
1/2 c bell pepper, chopped fine	2 c chicken broth
2 bundles green onions, chopped	salt, black pepper, and red (cayenne) pepper, to taste
1/2 celery, chopped fine	

Split shrimp and season with salt, black, and red pepper. Set aside. Melt butter or oil in heavy pot, add onions, celery, bell pepper, and garlic. Cook slowly, uncovered, until wilted. Add seasoned shrimp and let simmer, stirring constantly, for 20 minutes. Dissolve cornstarch in cold water and add to mixture with tomato paste. Cook another 15 minutes, stirring constantly. Add salt to taste. Serve over cooked rice.

Yield: 6–8 servings
Jacque Winnon Burchfield

" Worry about nothing, but pray about everything!"

CRAWFISH FETTUCCINI

2 large onions, chopped
1 bell pepper, chopped
1 1/4 sticks butter
1/2 c all purpose flour
1 1/2 c half and half
8-oz Cheez Whiz, regular
20-oz chicken broth

8-oz Cheez Whiz, jalapeño*
2 lbs crawfish tails**
1 tsp salt
1 tsp black pepper
1/2 tsp red pepper
2 tsp chopped garlic

Melt 3/4 stick butter and sauté onion and bell pepper. Melt remaining butter in separate container; add flour and cook until cream colored. Stir half and half, Cheez Whiz, chicken broth and seasonings into flour mixture. Add sautéed vegetables. Cook until Cheez Whiz is melted and mixture is smooth. Add crawfish. Cook on low heat for about 20 minutes. Serve over noodles or rice or with Melba toast or chips as a dip!

> *I can no longer find Cheez Whiz with jalapeño. I think Mexican Velveeta would probably work as well. I just used a tiny bit more red pepper in mine—it was a new can so it was fresh and hot.
> **This is also excellent with shrimp.

Marilyn S Winnon (Buddy)

FRIED SALMON

14 oz canned salmon
1/2 c sifted flour

1 egg, beaten
1 heaping tsp baking powder

Drain salmon into liquid measuring cup. Put into mixing bowl and flake, then add egg. Mix well with fork. Add flour and mix again. It will be thick. You can add pepper, but will not need salt. Use 1/4 c of the liquid and add the teaspoon of baking powder. Beat with a fork until it foams up. It should reach the 3/4 cup mark. Mix with salmon. Using two teaspoons, scoop some of the mixture out with one and with the other push it into a deep fryer half full of hot oil. Do not mix ahead of time. You may add garlic or onions.

Lillian Winnon Atkins

SALMON CROQUETTES

14-oz can pink salmon

1 egg, beaten

2 chopped scallions

1/4 c chopped parsley

1/2 c Italian seasoned bread crumbs

1/2 c cheddar or Swiss cheese, shredded

1 tbsp Worcestershire sauce

1 tbsp hot sauce

1 tbsp brown mustard

salt and pepper to taste

olive oil

SAUCE

1/4 brown mustard

1/4 c mayonnaise

salt and pepper

1 tsp olive oil

1/4 tsp cayenne

Drain salmon and remove skin and bones if desired. In large bowl, flake salmon and mix lightly with other ingredients. Shape into 3–4-inch patties. Fry in 1 inch of olive oil, about 3 minutes each side, until golden brown. Mix ingredients together for sauce and serve on the side.

John Atkins

SHRIMP ENCHILADAS

1/2 lb (2 sticks) unsalted butter, in all

1 c finely chopped onions

1 c canned green chilies, drained and chopped

3/4 c finely chopped green bell peppers

2 3/4 tsp salt, in all

2 3/4 tsp white pepper, in all

1/2 tsp ground red pepper (cayenne), in all

3/4 tsp dried oregano leaves, in all

1/2 tsp minced garlic

3 c heavy cream

1 c dairy sour cream

8 c (2 lb) grated Monterey Jack cheese, in all

2 lb peeled shrimp or crawfish

2/3 c finely chopped green onions

1/2 c vegetable oil

20 6-inch corn tortillas

In a large skillet melt 1 stick of butter. Add the onions, green chilies, bell peppers, 1 1/4 tsp salt, 3/4 tsp white pepper, 1/4 tsp red pepper, 1/4 tsp oregano, and garlic. Sauté over medium heat for 10 minutes, stirring often. Stir in heavy cream and bring mixture to a rapid boil. Reduce heat and simmer uncovered 10 minutes, stirring constantly. Add sour cream with a metal whisk. Beat continuously until the sour cream is dissolved, about 3 minutes. Add 3 cups of cheese and stir until melted. Set sauce aside. In a 4-quart saucepan melt the remaining 1 stick butter. Add the shrimp or crawfish, green onions, and remaining 1 1/2 tsp salt, 2 tsp white pepper, 1/4 tsp red pepper, and 1 tsp oregano. Sauté over medium heat for about 6 minutes, stirring occasionally. Add cheese sauce to the shrimp/crawfish mixture and stir well. Simmer 6–10 minutes, stirring occasionally. Set aside. Fill and roll enchiladas. Cover with sauce then 1/4 cup of cheese. Bake at 350°F, 5–8 minutes.

Jacque Winnon Burchfield

SHRIMP AND SPAGHETTI

1 c chopped onion

1 c chopped bell pepper

1 c chopped celery

1 stick butter

2 lb shrimp

1 can cream mushroom soup

1 large pkg thin
spaghetti, cooked

1 c cream shrimp soup

1 c cream of celery soup

1 large jar sliced mushrooms

1 can sliced black olives

1 lb jalapeño cheese

red pepper to taste

Sauté onions, bell pepper, and celery in butter. Add shrimp and sauté until pink. Add soup and stir slowly. Add mushrooms, olives, and jalapeño cheese. Cook over low fire until bubbly. (Caution: watch carefully, it will burn easily at this stage.) Add red pepper to taste and cooked spaghetti. Fold in, do not stir.

Jacque Winnon Burchfield

SEAFOOD NEUBERG

1/4 c margarine

2 tbsp cornstarch

1 tsp salt

1 tsp paprika

2 c cooked, diced lobster,
crabmeat, or cleaned cooked
shrimp

dash cayenne

2 c light cream

1/2 c dry sherry

2 egg yolks, beaten

Melt margarine in saucepan. Blend in cornstarch, salt, paprika, and cayenne. Remove from heat. Gradually blend in cream. Cook over medium heat. Stirring constantly until mixture comes to boil and boil 1 minute. Reduce heat. Gradually stir in sherry. Blend a little hot mixture into eggs, then stir all into remaining hot mixture in a saucepan. Add selected seafood. Heat, but do not boil. Serve over toast.

Makes about 6 servings
Lillian Winnon Atkins

TUNA CASSEROLE

3 tbsp chopped onion	1 tbsp lemon juice
3 tbsp bell pepper	1 can each cream of chicken and celery soup
1 tbsp melted oleo	2 c crushed potato chips
2 tbsp chopped pimento	2 7-oz cans of tuna
2/3 c milk	

Sauté onion and pepper in oleo for 3 minutes or until tender. Remove from heat. Combine other ingredients, mixing well. Line buttered casserole dish with potato chips. Add tuna mixture then top with chips and rest of mixture. Bake 350°F for 30 minutes.

Jacque Winnon Burchfield

BOBBY AND STEVE'S FRIED FISH

fish	Tony's seasoning
corn meal	peanut oil
salt	cooking thermometer
pepper	cast iron pot

Mae and Ivy Gene prepare fish for cooking, then we mix corn meal in Cajun shaker with seasoning—tasting to be sure it is just right. Pour oil in pot and heat on fish cooker outside to 300–350°F before dropping the fish in. Cook until fish is floating and golden brown (about 5–8 minutes depending on thickness of fish). Be sure to have 2 paper bags with paper towels in bottom to put in fish when done. Steve and Bob do taste testing to be sure they are just right before they can be served with hush puppies, baked potato, and cole slaw.

Bobby Mardis & Steve Winnon

MAE'S MAXIMS

" Love is like a butterfly. It goes where it pleases and it pleases where it goes."

VEGETABLES & SIDES

ASPARAGUS

Break and rinse and then place on the baking sheet. (I use either foil or parchment paper.) Then add salt and pepper, goat cheese, or whatever you have that sounds good, and drizzle on some olive oil. Bake at 400°F for about 13–15 minutes. Voilà! You can also add almonds or nuts if you like them. Sometimes I throw on mushrooms as well.

Kimberly Winnon AmRhein

TED'S BAKED BEANS

When employees eat at Vernon Sawyers this is the dish Ted is always asked to bring.

2 16-oz cans pork & beans	1 c barbecue sauce
1 lb pan hot sausage	1/2 c catsup
1/2 lb smoked sausage	1/4 c Worcestershire sauce
2 c chopped onion	1/4 c mustard
1 c chopped bell pepper	1/3 c brown sugar
2 tbsp chopped garlic	Tabasco or red pepper to taste

Thinly slice smoked sausage. Cook pan sausage & drain. Add onion, bell pepper & garlic to sausage & cook until tender. Mix all ingredients in a large baking dish & bake for 1 hour at 350°F. (Do not overcook.)

Ted Mardis

BROCCOLI CASSEROLE

2 c cooked rice	1 stick butter
2 pkg frozen broccoli	1 can cream of chicken soup
1 8-oz jar Cheez Whiz	1/4 medium onion, chopped

Sauté onion till tender in butter. Add soup, broccoli, and cheese. Simmer till broccoli is thawed. Add rice and place in baking dish. Bake for 30 minutes at 350°F.

Donna Winnon Cox

SMOTHERED CABBAGE

1 medium head of cabbage, cored and chopped

salt and pepper to taste

5 slices of bacon

Fry bacon in heavy pot. Add chopped cabbage. Cover. Stir occasionally (cabbage will brown in bacon drippings as the two cook together). Cook about 30 minutes. Salt and pepper to taste. Serve hot.

Jacque Winnon Burchfield

ITALIAN CABBAGE PATTIES

1 head cabbage, chopped

12 oz salt pork, sliced

2 eggs, room temp.

1/2 c Parmesan cheese

1/4 c Italian bread crumbs

1/4 c cooking oil

Place chopped cabbage and salt pork in a medium stock pot and cover with water. When done, drain and squeeze dry. In a mixing bowl, combine cabbage, eggs, cheese, and bread crumbs. Make into patties. Heat the oil over medium heat in a medium-sized frying pan. Fry patties until they are golden brown on both sides.

Jacque Winnon Burchfield

GLAZED CARROTS

1 lb carrots, cut in strips

1 small onion, chopped

1 c sugar

salt

2 tbsp butter

Cook carrots in water and salt until tender. Sauté onion in butter until clear. Add sugar. Cook slow until candied. Pour over drained carrots. Bake at 300°F for 15–20 minutes.

Jamie Winnon Rawls

CAULIFLOWER

Recipe from Al Klein

1 whole head of cauliflower, cut into small pieces

olive oil

1/2 stick of butter

garlic

1 onion, chopped

paprika

Parmesan cheese

Put cauliflower in a large frying pan with some olive oil and ¹/₂ stick of butter. Brown it down with some garlic, chopped onion, and paprika. After it is browned — and tender, put in large baking dish with some oil and butter and sprinkle it with Parmesan cheese and bake for 20–25 minutes to a golden brown.

Joan Winnon

EASY CORN CASSEROLE

This is a must dish for Morgan if she eats with me, at least if I don't have macaroni & cheese.

1 large can whole-kernel corn
1 large can cream-style corn
8 oz sour cream

1 box Jiffy cornbread mix
1 stick margarine, softened

Mix margarine and sour cream. Add cornbread mix, whole-kernel corn and cream-style corn. Stir until evenly mixed. Turn into casserole dish. Cook at 375°F for 45 minutes or until golden brown.

Mae Winnon Mardis

CORN AND CHEESE CASSEROLE

2 c fresh corn
1 c cheese
1 tbsp minced onion
¹/₂ c chopped green pepper

8 oz sour cream
1 stick oleo
1 pkg jalapeño cornbread mix

Combine all ingredients, stirring well. Spoon into a lightly greased 1-quart casserole. Cover and bake at 350°F for 30–40 minutes or until corn is tender.

Lillian Winnon Atkins

MEXICAN CORN CASSEROLE

2 cans cream corn
4 eggs, beaten
1 c Mexican cornbread mix
³/₄ c Wesson Oil

¹/₂ tsp garlic salt
1 small jar pimento
¹/₂ c grated cheese
3–4 green onions, chopped

Mix all ingredients together and pour into a 9x13 inch buttered casserole dish. Bake at 350°F for 45 minutes. Recipe can be cut in half for smaller casserole.

Donna Winnon Cox

FRIED CORN

2 c fresh corn
2 tbsp oil
salt and pepper

1 tbsp flour
1 c milk or cream

Sauté corn in oil until lightly browned, stirring often. Add flour and lightly brown. Pour in milk or cream and cook until thickened, adding more liquid for thinner mixture. Add salt and pepper to taste.

Ivy Gene Winnon

GREEK EGGPLANT WITH MEAT

A great way to use eggplant. Delicious!

2 medium-sized eggplants
$1/2$ c olive oil
2 tbsp instant onion
$1/4$ lb fresh mushrooms, sliced
$1/2$ lb ground beef

2 large tomatoes, peeled and chopped
2 tbsp melted butter

1 green pepper, cut into strips
$1/4$ tsp black pepper
$1/4$ tsp basil leaves
$1/8$ tsp nutmeg
1 c grated sharp cheddar cheese
$1/2$ c soft bread crumbs

Peel eggplant and cut into 1-inch-thick slices. In skillet, sauté eggplant in oil until lightly browned. Place in a single layer in 3-quart baking dish. Add onions and mushrooms to skillet and sauté until lightly browned. Stir in meat, tomatoes, green pepper, and seasonings.

Cover and simmer 5 minutes. Spoon meat mixture over eggplant. Sprinkle with cheese. Toss bread crumbs with butter and spoon over all. Bake in 350°F oven for 45 minutes.

Serves 6
Terri Winnon

GREEN STRING BEANS

6 slices bacon
3 c cut-up string beans
salt and pepper to taste

3 peeled medium potatoes
4 c water or more if necessary

Fry bacon; mix all ingredients together and cook until vegetables are tender. Serve hot.

Mae Winnon Mardis

GREEN BEAN WRAP

2 cans whole green beans	1 tbsp Worcestershire sauce, or to taste
1 stick butter	1 pkg bacon (thin sliced), cut in half
1 c light brown sugar	toothpicks

Drain green beans. In boiler combine brown sugar, butter, Worcestershire sauce, and melt into sauce. Wrap 4–5 green beans in half-slices of bacon. Stick toothpicks in to hold together. Place wrapped beans on cookie sheet and pour sauce over them. Cook at 350°F about 30 minutes.

Morgan Watson Johnston

KIM'S BEANS

These are a meal in themselves . . . this recipe also doubles/triples well for a BBQ or big party. I also do these in the crockpot for big BBQs, and they turn out great!!

1/2 lb hamburger, browned	1/4 c ketchup
1/2 lb bacon, fried and chopped	1/3 c brown sugar
1 onion, diced	1/3 c white sugar
1 can butter beans, drained	1 tbsp spicy brown mustard
1 can kidney beans, drained	2 tbsp molasses
1 can pork and beans (do not drain)	

Mix all ingredients and bake for 1 hour at 350°F.

Kimberly Winnon AmRhein

OKRA AND TOMATO

4 c sliced okra	1 tbsp sugar
1 c sliced onion	1 tsp salt
1/4 c olive oil	1 tsp black pepper
4 or 5 large tomatoes, peeled and cut up or 1 can stewed tomatoes	red pepper to taste or fresh hot pepper from garden

Sauté onions in half of the oil to heat well. Remove and add remaining oil. Add okra and cook until no longer slimy. You may have to add a little more oil. Keep stirred so okra doesn't burn. The quicker it cooks, the better, so okra won't be mushy. Add tomatoes, sugar, salt, pepper, and onions; simmer until tomatoes and okra are tender and cooked down. Good with fresh or dried beans or peas.

Ivy Gene Hamby Winnon

ONION RINGS

onions	flour
milk	Wesson Oil

Cut onions into 1/4-inch slices and separate into rings. Dip in milk, then into flour. Fry until golden brown in deep oil heated to 375°F. Drain and salt.

Lillian Winnon Atkins

SQUASH DRESSING

From Mattie Moore

1 package Mexican cornbread mix	1 egg
5 or 6 squash	1 can cream of chicken soup
1 onion, chopped	1/2 stick margarine

Bake Mexican cornbread mix according to package. Cook squash with the chopped onion together until tender. Mash the squash and onion. Melt the 1/2 stick of margarine, and add to squash. Add the egg and the cream of chicken soup. Add the crumbled corn bread. Bake at 350°F for 30 to 35 minutes. Good . . .

Joan Winnon

SQUASH DRESSING

2 c cooked squash, drained	2 c crumbled cornbread
1/2 c margarine	1 can cream of chicken soup
1 onion, chopped	salt and pepper to taste
1 bunch green onion, chopped	

Cook squash until tender. Sauté onion in margarine. Mix all ingredients together and pour into casserole dish. Bake for 30–40 minutes.

> Variations: Add 1 cup cooked chicken or 1 pound browned sausage. Substitute eggplant for squash.

Mae Winnon Mardis

FRIED GREEN TOMATOES

3 or 4 green tomatoes, sliced 1/4 in thick	1/4 c flour
salt	Tony's seasoning to taste
1/2 c cornmeal	1 egg white, beaten slightly

Lightly salt the tomato slices and let them drain a few minutes. Mix together the dry ingredients. Dip the slices in egg white, then in dry mix. Heavy coating makes them better. Fry in black iron skillet over medium-high heat until brown and crusty. Drain on paper towel.

Mae Winnon Mardis

VEGETABLE CASSEROLE

This recipe came to me from Mrs. Daisy (Granny) Calhoun—we go to the same church.

2 16-oz cans Veg-All	1 c mayonnaise
1 8-oz can water chestnuts, sliced	1 stick oleo
1 c chopped onion	1 pkg Ritz crackers

Mix first 4 ingredients. Put in baking dish. Melt oleo and pour over crushed Ritz crackers. Mix. Put on top of other ingredients. Bake 35 minutes at 350°F.

Mae Winnon Mardis

POTATO CASSEROLE

6 to 8 medium potatoes	8 oz Velveeta cheese
1 medium onion	4 oz sour cream
1/2 stick margarine	1 c grated cheddar cheese
1 can cream chicken soup	salt and pepper

Boil potatoes in jackets and cool. Sauté onions in margarine until clear (not brown). Add soup and cheese until smooth, then add sour cream. Peel potatoes and slice thin. Layer potatoes and cheese mixture and grated cheddar cheese. Sprinkle potatoes with salt and pepper as you layer them. End layers with cheddar cheese. Bake 300°F until cheese is melted and casserole bubbly. About 45 minutes.

Serves 6 to 8
Jamie Winnon Rawls

POTATO CASSEROLE

4 or 5 potatoes, peeled, boiled and drained	1/2 c milk
1/2 c sour cream	1/2–1 c mild shredded cheddar cheese
1 stick butter	2–3 tbsp potato toppers

Mix potatoes, milk, and butter to make mashed potatoes. Add sour cream, cheese, and potato toppers. Mix well. Place in casserole dish. Sprinkle with potato toppers. Bake at 350°F for 10–20 minutes to melt cheese.

Cissie Winnon Purvis

HASH BROWN POTATO CASSEROLE

1 32-oz bag of hash browns	1 8-oz sour cream
1/2 c melted margarine	1 tsp salt
1 can cream of chicken soup	1 small onion
12 oz grated American cheese	2 c crushed corn flakes

Place thawed potatoes in casserole dish. Mix rest of ingredients and put in casserole with hash brown potatoes. Top with corn flakes and drizzle with margarine. Bake 350°F for 45 minutes.

Joan Winnon

HASH BROWN CASSEROLE

1 bag hash browns	1/4 c white onions
1 can cream of mushroom soup	2 c shredded cheese
1 can cream of chicken soup	1 jar bacon bits
1/4 c green onions	8 oz sour cream

Mix all ingredients together. Sprinkle with a little garlic salt and Tony's. Bake at 375°F until done.

Brenda Winnon Myers

CALIFORNIA POTATOES CASSEROLE

2 lbs frozen hashbrown potatoes	2 c shredded Parmesan cheese
1 pt sour cream	2–3 cans cream of chicken soup or any other cream soup desired
1/2 c melted margarine or butter	salt and pepper, to taste
1/4 c freeze-dried onions	

Mix all ingredients together and place in a 9x13-inch baking pan.

TOPPING

1 pkg Ritz crackers, crushed	1/2 c melted butter or margarine

Mix together butter and crackers and spread on the potato mixture. Bake uncovered at 350°F for approximately 30–45 minutes.

Jacque Winnon Burchfield

CHEESY SCALLOPED POTATOES

2 cans cream of celery or cream of mushroom soup	1 c thinly sliced onion
1/2 c milk	2 c shredded sharp cheddar cheese
1/4 tsp pepper	1 tbsp butter
8 c thinly sliced potatoes	paprika

Combine soup, milk, and pepper. In 2 1/2-inch shallow baking dish arrange alternate layers of potatoes, onions, cheese and soup mixture. Dot top with butter and sprinkle with paprika. Cover and bake at 375°F for 1 hour. Uncover and bake 15 minutes more or until done.

8 servings
Mae Winnon Mardis

MY MOTHER'S OVEN-BAKED POTATOES

This was my mother Dorothy Belton's recipe.

6 medium potatoes, well scrubbed	1 large onion, cut into small chunks
1/4 c oleo	1 garlic clove, split
salt, pepper, celery seed, and paprika	

Cut unpeeled potatoes into 1 1/2 in chunks. Arrange in single layer in shallow pan with onion chunks tucked into potatoes. Melt butter with garlic halves. Remove garlic, and drizzle butter over potatoes. Sprinkle layer with salt, pepper, celery seed. Cover with foil and bake 45 minutes in a 400°F oven. Remove foil, sprinkle with paprika, and continue baking for about 20 minutes until browned.

Terri Winnon

TWICE-BAKED STUFFED POTATOES

4–6 med/large white russet potatoes	potato toppers
1 can white claw crabmeat (drained)	mild cheddar cheese
1 8-oz carton sour cream	milk
butter	salt
pepper	

Bake potatoes until done. Wrap in aluminum foil and let cool for about 20–30 minutes. Unwrap potatoes (save foil). Cut potatoes in half. Spoon out potato and put in bowl. Save potato peel halves. Add butter, sour cream, and small amount of milk JUST to help mix easier. Add drained crabmeat, cheese, potato toppers, salt and pepper to taste. Mixture should be slightly moist but not runny. Fill each side of potato with mixture. Carefully put potatoes back together and wrap in foil. (Mixture will be coming out on sides.) Heat in oven on 350°F for 20–30 minutes.

Cissie Winnon Purvis

CANDIED SWEET POTATOES

This is Al's Mothers recipe. Everyone loves it.

3–4 medium sweet potatoes, cut in thin julienne strips

1/4 c water

1 1/2 c white sugar

1/2 stick butter

1/4 tbsp vanilla

1/4 tbsp butter flavor

sprinkle with apple pie spice

Cover and cook on medium heat until tender and juicy. Take lid off and cook on very low fire until done. Do not stir too much or potatoes will be mushy and not candied.

Jamie Winnon Rawls

SWEET POTATO CASSEROLE

3 c sweet potatoes

1/2 c butter

1 tsp vanilla

1/2 c sugar

2 eggs, beaten

1/3 c milk

Boil and mash potatoes. Mix in sugar, butter, eggs, vanilla, and milk. Put in 13x9-inch baking dish.

TOPPING

1/2 c melted butter

1/2 c flour

1 c light brown sugar

1 c chopped pecans

Melt butter and mix in remaining ingredients. Sprinkle on top of potato mixture. Bake 25 minutes at 350°F.

Serves 10 to 12
Jamie Winnon Rawls

BAKED RICE

2 tbsp vegetable oil	1 tbsp butter
1 c uncooked rice	1/4 c fresh mushrooms, sliced
1/4 c chopped onion	1/4 tbsp salt
2 c chicken broth	1/4 tsp sage (optional)

Heat oil in large cast-iron skillet. Add rice. Brown. Add onion. Cook until clear. Add mushrooms, then broth. Stir in rice. Cover and bake at 350°F for 30 minutes.

Jamie Winnon Rawls

LOUISIANA RED BEANS AND RICE

1 c red beans, washed and drained	1 large bay leaf, crushed
3 c water	1 clove garlic
1 stalk celery, chopped	1 medium onion, chopped

Cook beans in water. Season with salt and bacon drippings, ham, or dry salt pork. Cook for 1 1/2 hours. Add onion, garlic, celery, and bay leaf. Continue to cook over low heat for 1 hour. If beans become too dry, add hot water. Two tbsp of sugar may be added. Cook rice by favorite recipe. Serve over rice and with cornbread.

Lillian Winnon Atkins

HOMEMADE RICE PILAF

1/2 c spaghetti, broken into approx. 1/2-inch pieces	1 tbsp onion, minced
5 tbsp butter	1 chicken bouillon cube
1 c long grain rice	2 c water

Melt butter in skillet or 3-quart saucepan. Stir in broken spaghetti and sauté until golden brown. Add long-grain rice and onions. Cook until onions are translucent. Stir in 2 cups water and bouillon cube. Bring to boil and then reduce heat to low. Cover and cook for 25 minutes. Serve as side dish with poultry or fish.

Joyce Atkins Keller

RAVISHING RICE

This recipe was given to me by Faye Crnkovic, who is Vicki Mardis' mom. It is quick, easy, and good.

1 bell pepper chopped

1 onion chopped

celery amount your choice

1 lb sausage cooked and drained

5 c water

2 pkg dry chicken noodle soup

1 c rice

Cook and drain sausage. Add chopped ingredients and sauté. Stir dry chicken noodle soup and rice into 5 cups water and boil for 10 minutes. Mix sausage group with soup and rice in casserole dish. Cook about 30 minutes until bubbly at 350°F.

Mae Winnon Mardis

RICE & CORN CASSEROLE

1 5-oz package of yellow rice

1 can cream of celery soup

cheddar cheese

1 can Mexican corn

1 stick butter

Cook yellow rice, but don't add butter. When the rice is done, add butter, soup, and corn in a casserole dish. Cover mixture with cheddar cheese and bake at 350°F until done.

8 servings
Joan Winnon

WHITE/WILD RICE CASSEROLE

1 box Uncle Ben's white/wild rice

1 onion, chopped

3 celery stalks, chopped

slivered almonds (optional)

1 can French green beans, drained

2 c chicken, chopped*

1 can water chestnuts, chopped and drained

1 can cream of mushroom soup

1 can mushrooms, drained and chopped

Cook rice as directed on the box. Sauté the onion and celery together. Add almonds if desired. Stir in chicken, water chestnuts, soup, mushrooms, and green beans. Sprinkle paprika on top. Bake at 350°F for 30 minutes.

*Broasted chicken from Sam's is good.

8 Servings
Joan Winnon

BREADS, ROLLS & PASTRIES

PANCAKES

1 egg, well beaten
1 1/4 c sweet milk
2 tbsp sugar

2 tbsp vegetable oil
1 1/4 c self-rising flour

Mix ingredients and beat until smooth. Pour onto griddle and cook until brown. Flip and brown the other side.

Donna Winnon Cox

CHEESE BISCUITS

2 c all-purpose flour
3 tsp baking powder

1/2 tsp salt

1/2 c shortening
1 c (4 oz) shredded sharp
cheddar cheese
2/3 c milk

Combine flour, baking powder, and salt; cut in shortening and cheese until mixture resembles coarse meal. Add milk, stirring until moistened. Turn dough out onto a lightly floured surface and kneed lightly 3 or 4 times. Roll dough to 1/2-inch thickness. Cut into rounds with a 2-inch cutter. Place biscuits on a lightly greased baking sheet; bake at 450°F for 8–10 minutes.

Yield: About 1 1/2 dozen
Jamie Winnon Rawls

QUICK CHEESE BISCUITS

2 c Pioneer buttermilk
baking mix
2/3 c milk

1/2 tsp garlic powder

1/2 c shredded cheddar cheese

2 tbsp butter/margarine,
melted

Mix biscuit mix, milk, and cheese until moist. Drop by tablespoon onto ungreased baking sheet. Mix butter and garlic powder together. Brush over biscuits. Bake at 475°F for 8–10 minutes or until golden brown. (Better if butter is added after baked.)

Cissie Winnon Purvis

* June Winnon Dawkins

Mama (Aunt Beattie) told the story of the first time she attempted to make biscuits. Somehow, the dough didn't work out, so she took it outside and buried it in the yard to hide it from Daddy (Uncle Pete). By the time he came in from the fields for lunch, the sun had heated up the buried dough and it was pushing up from its burial site. She could see a white swell coming out of the ground and the chickens were pecking it. So much for hiding it from Daddy!!!

CHEESY SAUSAGE BISCUITS

3 c biscuit mix

1–1½ c grated cheddar cheese

2 lb pan sausage, browned

1½ c buttermilk

Combine biscuit mix, sausage, and cheese with enough buttermilk to make a stiff dough. Spray pans with Pam. Roll out biscuits 2–3 inches in diameter. Place in pans and spray tops with Pam. Bake at 400°F until light brown.

Note: The more cheese used, the flatter the biscuit will be.

Mae Winnon Mardis

CHEESE BREAD

1 c butter

2 c sugar

2 c boiling water

2 tsp garlic salt

2 pkg yeast

2 beaten eggs

6 c plain flour

Melt butter and add sugar, 1 cup of boiling water, and garlic salt. Let cool. Dissolve 2 packages yeast in 1 cup of boiling water. Add to first mixture. Add eggs and plain flour. Let rise 4 hours in refrigerator. (Sometimes I make up at night and put in refrigerator until morning.) Divide in 4 equal parts. Roll into jellyroll rectangle, dot with cheese, roll, and tuck ends. Let rise 1 hour in draft-free place. Brush with butter. Bake 350°F until brown, or if you put in freezer, do not brown. Warm in oven.

Jamie Winnon Rawls

CHEESE BREAD

loaf of French bread, sliced
Monterey Jack cheese, grated
oregano leaves

mayonnaise
garlic powder*

Mix cheese, garlic powder and oregano with enough mayonnaise to make a spreadable consistency. Spread on French bread slices. Place under broiler until cheese is bubbly. Always a big hit.

*I did not use the garlic powder because Lynn doesn't like it.
Marilyn S Winnon (Buddy)

BANANA BREAD

1 c sugar
1/4 c Crisco
2 eggs
3 bananas, mashed

1 1/2 c all-purpose flour
1 tsp baking soda
1/2 tsp salt

Blend sugar and Crisco. Then add eggs and mashed bananas. Add in flour, soda and salt. Mix well and pour into greased baking pan. Bake at 350°F for about 1 hour.

Yield: 12 servings
Jacque Winnon Burchfield

DEBI BROWN'S BANANA BREAD

1 c sugar
1/4 c Crisco
2 eggs
3 bananas, mashed

1 1/2 c plain flour
1 tsp baking soda
1/2 tsp salt

Blend sugar and Crisco. Add eggs and bananas, then the flour, soda, and salt. Cream all together and then pour into a greased loaf pan. Bake at 350°F for about 1 hour.

Makes 12 servings
Joan Winnon

COCONUT BREAD

Given to me by Lola Eppinette.

4 eggs
2 c sugar
2 tsp coconut flavoring
1/2 tsp salt
1 c pecans, chopped
1 c oil

3 c flour
1/2 tsp baking powder
1/2 tsp baking soda
1 c buttermilk
2 c coconut

Beat eggs in a large bowl. Add sugar, oil, and coconut flavoring. Blend well. Sift dry ingredients together; add alternately with buttermilk to the egg mixture. Fold in coconut and nuts. Pour into 2 9 1/2 x 5 1/2 x 3-inch greased and floured pans. Bake at 325°F for approximately 60 minutes or until done. For glass pans, bake at 300°F.

TOPPING

2 c sugar	1 c water
4 tbsp butter	2 tsp coconut flavoring

Combine sugar, butter, and water in saucepan. Cook 5 minutes. Add coconut flavoring. Pour over hot bread after it is removed from oven. Let stand 4 hours.

Yield: 2 loaves
Mae Winnon Mardis

SAUSAGE BREAD

1 lb sausage	1 block jalapeño cheese (or whatever cheese you prefer)
1 can Pillsbury French loaf bread	

Brown sausage and drain. Spray baking sheet with Pam. Roll out French loaf bread and fill with sausage and sliced cheese. Roll up into loaf; press ends under. Bake at 375°F for about 20–30 minutes.

Brenda Winnon Myers

CAJUN SAUSAGE BREAD

1 lb hot sausage	1/3 c bell peppers, chopped
2 or 3 cloves garlic chopped or garlic powder	2–3 jalapeño peppers, finely chopped
3 c grated cheddar cheese	3 tbsp melted butter
1 1/2 c green onions, chopped, tops and all	2 16-oz leaves frozen bread dough

Cook sausage and garlic, in skillet over medium heat. Remove and drain on paper towels. In medium bowl, combine sausage, cheese, onions, bell peppers, and chilies. Grease 2 baking sheets or 1 large pan.

On floured board, roll out each dough piece to a 9x13-inch rectangle. Spread half the sausage mixture evenly over each piece, leaving a half-inch border. Roll up as for a jellyroll. Let rise 45 minutes to 1 hour. Then brush with melted margarine. Bake at 350°F until golden brown, about 35–40 minutes.

Jacque Winnon Burchfield
& Ivy Gene Winnon

HAWAIIAN BREAD

2 c chopped ham

16 oz sharp grated cheese

8 oz cream cheese

8 oz sour cream

1 pan Hawaiian bread

1/2 c minced green onion tops

1 4 1/2-oz can green chilies, chopped

1 tsp Worcestershire sauce

1 tsp hot sauce

Cut top out of bread; hollow out. Save bread pieces to dip with. Mix all ingredients well; stuff in bread. Bake at 350°F, covered with foil, for 40 minutes. Uncover and bake 20 more minutes. Serve with bread pieces or party crackers.

Mae Winnon Mardis

ZUCCHINI BREAD

This freezes well and that is good because when you raise squash, there is usually an overabundance and needs to be used one way or another. NEVER WASTE.

1 1/2 c flour

1/4 tsp salt

1/2 tsp baking soda

1 tsp baking powder

3/4 tsp cinnamon

3/4 c sugar

2 eggs

1/2 c oil

2 tsp vanilla

1 1/2 c zucchini or yellow squash coarsely shredded and lightly packed

Preheat oven to 350°F. Grease loaf pan. Mix all dry ingredients except sugar. Beat eggs until frothy. Add sugar, oil, and vanilla. Beat until lemon color, about 3 minutes. Stir in shredded squash. Add dry ingredients. Mix well just until moistened. Pour into pan. Bake about 40 minutes or until toothpick inserted in center comes out clean. Cool about 10 minutes before removing from pan.

Mae Winnon Mardis

OLD-FASHION BLUEBERRY MUFFINS

2 c all-purpose flour

2/3 c sugar

1 tbsp baking powder

1/2 tsp salt

1/2 c melted butter

1 dash apple pie spice

1 1/2 c blueberries

2 beaten eggs

1/2 c milk

Combine all dry ingredients. Toss blueberries in 1/4 cup flour. Make a well in center of mixture. Combine eggs, milk, and butter. Add to dry ingredients. Fold blueberries into mixture. Spoon into greased muffin tins, filling 2/3 full. Bake at 400°F for 18–20 minutes.

Sometimes I add 1/2 cup pecans for variety.

Makes 18 muffins
Jamie Winnon Rawls

CINNAMON ROLLS

1/2 c warm water	2 eggs, beaten
2 pkg active dry yeast	1 tsp salt
1 tbsp granulated sugar	8 c all-purpose flour
1 3 1/2-oz pkg instant vanilla pudding	1/2 c butter, melted
2 c milk	1+ c sugar
1/2 c butter, melted	1/4 c good quality cinnamon

In a small bowl, combine water, yeast and sugar. Stir until dissolved. Set aside. In large bowl, make pudding mix according to package directions. Add butter, eggs and salt: mix well. Add the yeast mixture. Blend. Gradually add flour and knead until smooth and elastic. Place in a very large greased bowl. Cover and let rise until double (about 1 hour). Punch down and let rise again (45 minutes). On lightly floured surface, roll out to a 1/4-inch-thick rectangle, 21 inches in its smaller dimension.

Note: You may wish to divide the dough in halves and roll out two rectangles. You may have to partially roll it out, then cover it with a damp cloth and let it rest before finishing.

Spread 1/2 cup melted butter over surface. Mix cinnamon and sugar together, and spread evenly over surface, leaving a 1-inch margin along one of the long edges. Roll up tightly, starting from a long side. Press together along the edge not covered with cinnamon sugar. Slice at 1 1/2-inch intervals. Place on greased baking pan, approximately 2 inches apart. Cover and let rise until double again. Bake at 350°F for 15–20 minutes. Remove as soon as they turn golden. Frost warm rolls with cream cheese frosting.

CREAM CHEESE FROSTING

1 4-oz cream cheese, room temperature	1 1/2 tsp milk
1/4 c butter, softened	3 tbsp real maple syrup
1 1/2 c powdered sugar	1/2 c raisins (optional)
1/2 tsp vanilla	1/2 c walnuts (optional)

Blend ingredients together and spread over rolls. Add small amount of walnuts and raisins if desired.

Joyce Atkins Keller

CARAMEL ROLLS

2 loaves frozen bread dough, defrosted

1/2 c butter or margarine

1 tsp cinnamon

1 c brown sugar, packed

1 small package regular vanilla pudding mix

In a medium pan, melt butter and mix in brown sugar, pudding mix, and cinnamon. Cut with scissors 1 loaf of bread into a Bundt pan. Pour warm caramel mixture over bread. Cut up the second loaf of bread over the caramel layer. Let rise.

Bake at 325°F for 30 minutes. Let cool slightly before turning out onto cake platter.

Joyce Atkins Keller

PECAN ROLLS

1 7-oz jar marshmallow cream

1 1-lb package powdered sugar

1 tsp vanilla extract

1 14-oz pkg assorted vanilla and chocolate caramels

3 tbsp water

1 to 1 1/2 c chopped pecans

Combine first 3 ingredients, mixing well with hands. Shape mixture into 5 4x1-inch rolls—mixture will be very dry. Chill 2–3 hours.

Combine caramels and water in top of a double boiler; cook until melted. Dip rolls in melted caramel, and roll each in pecans. Chill 1 hour. Cut into slices to serve.

Yield: 5 rolls
Terri Winnon

MONKEY BREAD

3 cans biscuits

1 tbsp cinnamon

1/2 c sugar

1 stick oleo

1 c brown sugar

2 tsp water

1/2 c nuts

Quarter biscuits; roll in cinnamon and sugar that have been mixed together. Put in greased Bundt pan. (Optional: Place nuts in bottom of pan before adding biscuits.) Melt oleo; add brown sugar and water; boil 2 minutes and pour over biscuits. Bake at 350°F for 25 minutes.

Melinda Mardis Bryan

ICE BOX ROLLS

1 qt warm milk   1/2 c sugar
1 or 2 pkg yeast   3/4 c oil

Add enough flour to make a thick dough. Let rise approximately 2 hour. Punch down, cover, and store in refrigerator. Use as needed.

Lillian Winnon Atkins

90-MINUTE DINNER ROLLS

2 –2 1/2 c unsifted flour   1/2 c milk
2 tbsp sugar   1/4 c water
1/2 tsp salt   2 tbsp margarine
1 pkg active dry yeast

Mix 3/4 cup flour, sugar, salt, and undissolved yeast. Heat milk, water, and margarine to 120–130°F. Gradually add to dry ingredients and beat 2 minutes at medium speed of mixer. Add 1/4 cup flour. Beat at high speed 2 minutes. Stir in enough additional flour to make soft dough. On floured board kneed 2–3 minutes. Divide dough into 12 equal pieces. Shape into balls. Place in greased 8-inch round pan. Pour a 1-inch depth of boiling water into large pan on bottom rack of cold oven. Set rolls on rack above water. Cover. Close oven door. Let rise 30 minutes. Uncover rolls. Remove pan of water. Turn oven to 375°F. Bake 20–25 minutes or until done. Remove from pan to cool. Serve warm.

Makes 1 dozen
Cissie Winnon Purvis

PINECREST SCHOOL CAFETERIA ROLLS

3 1/2 lbs plain flour   1 c dry milk
1 qt warm water   1/8 c salt
1 1/2 c oil   1 c sugar
1/4 c yeast

Mix 3 lbs of flour, sugar, dry milk, and salt together. Add this to mixer with 1 quart of warm water and 1 1/2 cups of oil. Mix until all dry ingredients are mixed in. Then add remaining 1/2 lb flour and 1/4 cup yeast to this. Beat until mixture pulls away from sides of bowl. Let rise in bowl for about 30 minutes. Mixture should double in size to be ready. Pinch off and make size rolls you like and place on greased cookie sheet. Set in warm place and let rise again. Brush tops of rolls with melted butter. Bake at 325°F till browned. These may be frozen. When ready to use, take desired amount out and place rolls on lightly greased baking pan. Allow dough to thaw and rise in a warm place free of drafts until dough doubles in size (approximately 2 hours). Bake as directed above.

Brenda Winnon Myers

CORNBREAD

1/4 c self-rising flour	3/4 c self-rising yellow cornmeal
1 egg	1-1 1/4 c milk

Heat oven to 450°F. Warm small amount of oil in pan. Mix all ingredients together, then add warm oil in batter. Stir well. Pour batter in hot greased pan. Cook until brown.

MAE'S CORNBREAD

2 c cornmeal	Pinch baking soda
1/2 c flour	1/2 c milk
1 tsp salt	1 egg
1 tbsp baking powder	water

Before you begin set oven 450°F. Mix all dry ingredients in bowl. Pour some cooking oil in baking pan and put in oven to heat. (My Mama told me one time that the secret to good bread was a hot oven and hot pan.) Add milk and egg and stir. Add enough water making it to the consistency you want. Pour in hot pan with oil and place in oven to cook about 20–25 minutes until good and brown. When done the corners are good to slice, butter, and eat.

Mae Winnon Mardis

MAMA'S CORNBREAD

Mama made this for Daddy EVERY DAY!!!! Mama never measured anything, so I had to get her to "dump" each handful into an empty bowl so I could transfer it to a measuring cup to get the correct measurements!!!

1/2 c flour	1 tsp salt
1 c corn meal	1 egg
1 tsp baking powder	milk, enough to allow mixture to pour into skillet

Mix all above together. Heat one tablespoonful of bacon grease in an 8-inch cast iron skillet until very hot, making sure grease is swirled around in skillet to cover bottom and sides. Pour mixture into hot skillet. Bake at 400°F for approximately 25 minutes or until done.

June Winnon Dawkins

" Get all you can.
Can all you get.
Then sit on the can."

HOT-WATER CORNBREAD

This cornbread is a must for Troy (grandson) when I cook peas. Don't think he could eat the peas without it.

1 1/2 c self-rising cornmeal

1/2 c self-rising flour

boiling water

1 tbsp sugar (optional)

jalapeño slices (optional)

Mix dry ingredients. Stir in boiling water until it forms a stiff dough. When cool enough to handle, with wet hands, mold into patties and fry in deep oil until lightly browned. Drain on paper towels.

Mae Winnon Mardis

BLACK-EYED CORNBREAD

1 lb pork sausage

1 onion

1 c cornmeal

1/2 c flour

1 tsp salt

1/2 tsp soda

2 c black-eyed peas

2 eggs

1 c buttermilk

1/3 c oil

chopped green chilies

3/4 c creamed corn

8 oz cheddar cheese

Sauté sausage and onion, drain, and set aside. Combine dry ingredients. Then add all ingredients together. Cook at 350°F.

Jamie Winnon Rawls

CRAWFISH CORNBREAD

1 c yellow cornmeal

1/2 tbsp salt

1/2 tsp baking soda

1/2 tbsp baking powder

3 eggs

1 onion

1/4 c jalapeño

8 oz cheddar cheese

1/4 c bell pepper

1/3 c oil

1 large can cream corn

1 lb crawfish tails

Combine dry ingredients. Beat eggs and all other ingredients. Mix with dry ingredients. Bake in 9x13-inch pan at 375°F until done.

Melinda Mardis Bryan

MEXICAN CORNBREAD

1 1/2 c cornmeal
1 c sour cream
2 eggs
1 tsp salt
2 tbsp minced bell pepper

1 can cream-style corn
1/2 c salad oil
3 tsp baking powder
2 jalapeño peppers, chopped
1 c sharp cheddar cheese, grated

Mix all ingredients except cheese. Pour half of mixture into hot greased iron skillet. Sprinkle half of cheese over this. Add remaining mix and cover with cheese. Bake at 350°F for 40 minutes.

Lillian Winnon Atkins

CORNBREAD DRESSING

1 hen
salt, pepper, and sage
cool cornbread

2 c chicken broth

1 c chopped celery
1 c chopped onion

1 c grated carrots
1 stick butter
1 can cream of chicken & mushroom soup
1 pkg Pepperidge Farm Herb seasoning mix
4–6 eggs slightly beaten

Cook hen with salt, pepper and small amount of sage to get best chicken broth. Cook cornbread as directed on Aunt Jemima Yellow Cornmeal. Cool cornbread completely. (I usually save cornbread in freezer a few weeks before holidays.) In a saucepan, cook celery, onions, carrots, and butter in chicken broth until tender. Crumble cornbread and 1 package Pepperidge Farm Herb seasoning mix. Add eggs, vegetables, and soup. Mix well. Add chicken. Bake 350°F until done, about 1 1/2 hours.

Jamie Winnon Rawls

CORNBREAD DRESSING

1 cooked hen (the more natural chicken fat the better the dressing)
salt and pepper
4 eggs

The Trinity of the South:

1 large bell pepper, chopped
4 stalks of celery, chopped

sage	2 medium onions, chopped
1 c flour	1 large pan cooked cornbread (best if one day old)
1 c cooking oil	

Cook together until chicken is done. Save broth. Debone chicken.

Make a large pan of cornbread with yellow cornmeal. Crumble cornbread in large mixing bowl. Mix chicken broth with cornbread until mix is very wet (not like batter, but some liquid floats). Make sure all the cooked trinity is in the wet dressing if all the broth is not used.

Salt and pepper to taste. Add 2 raw eggs to mixture. Add sage—start with 2 tsp, add more if needed.

Set aside one cup uncooked dressing mixture and remaining broth.

Mix deboned chicken into dressing mixture. Place mixture in large pan. (Pan can be filled almost to top. This mixture will not increase in size.) Bake in 400°F oven until mixture is firm and golden brown on top.

Boil 2 eggs. Make roux with equal amount of oil and flour. Cook roux until light brown stirring continually—don't let it burn. Pour in remaining broth to make gravy. Chopped boiled eggs and add to gravy. Serve gravy over cooked dressing. Enjoy.

Lillian Winnon Atkins

CROCKPOT DRESSING

1 large skillet cornbread	3 sticks celery, chopped
3 slices bread	1 bunch green onion, chopped
1 cooked chicken, deboned	4 c chicken broth
1 can cream of celery soup	4 eggs, beaten
2 cans cream of chicken soup	butter (approximately 1 tbsp)

Crumble breads. Place celery and onions in boiler. Cover with some of broth. Cook 5 minutes. While this is cooking mix cream of chicken and cream of celery to breads. Add beaten eggs and chicken broth. Mix well. Add onion and celery to mixture. Add sage to taste. Put half of dressing mixture in crockpot. Add chicken, then put other half of dressing on top of chicken. Place pats of butter on top. (This will keep it from drying out while cooking.) Cook on high for 2 hours and then on low for 2 1/2 hours.

Lillian Phillips

HUSH PUPPIES

1 c self-rising cornmeal
1/3 c self-rising flour
1/4 c onion
1 can cream-style corn

3 green onions, chopped
1 egg
1/2 tsp salt
1 tbsp jalapeño peppers, chopped (optional)

Mix dry ingredients, egg, and corn so that mixture sticks together. Mix well. Drop by spoonfuls into hot oil. Cook until golden brown.

Lillian Winnon Atkins

HUSH PUPPIES

2 c corn meal mix
1 4-oz can cream corn
1 egg

1 onion, chopped
2 jalapeño peppers, chopped
buttermilk

Combine all ingredients except buttermilk in mixing bowl. Add only enough buttermilk to make a stiff batter. Drop by teaspoons of batter into hot oil; fry till done.

Ivy Gene Hamby Winnon

HUSH PUPPIES

1 egg
3 tbsp flour
7–8 tbsp corn meal
1 tsp baking powder
1 tsp salt
1/2 can cream style corn

cheddar cheese, grated
1 onion, chopped
dash garlic salt
1/4 c powdered milk
3–4 jalapeño peppers

Mix ingredients well. Deep fry in oil (not too hot).

Jacque Winnon Burchfield

HUSH PUPPIES

1 c yellow corn meal
1/2 c self-rising flour
1 tbsp baking powder
1/2 c chopped onion

1/2 tbsp sugar
1 egg
3/4 c buttermilk

Mix well, then add egg and buttermilk just before ready to put in hot grease. These will turn over themselves. Cook until brown and floating.

Jamie Winnon Rawls

SQUASH PUPPIES

2 c cooked squash	1 tsp baking powder
1 egg, beaten	1/4 c flour
1 onion, chopped	1/2 c buttermilk
3/4 c corn meal	salt and pepper to taste

Cook squash until tender. Drain and mash. Add remaining ingredients and drop by teaspoonfuls into hot oil. Cook until light brown and done on inside. Turning as necessary.

Jacque Winnon Burchfield

GARLIC GRITS

1 c quick-cooking grits	1/4 c evaporated milk
1/2 stick butter	1 6-oz roll garlic cheese
Tabasco	

Cook grits according to directions on package. Remove from heat. Add butter, milk, cheese, and dash of Tabasco. Mix together. Transfer to baking dish and bake at 375°F for 30 minutes.

Jacque Winnon Burchfield

JAMIE'S LITTLE PIZZA

1/2 c cheddar cheese, shredded	1/2 c green salad olives, chopped
1/2 c Monterey Jack cheese, shredded	1 tbsp chili powder
1/3 c real mayonnaise	

Mix well. Spread on English muffin bread or round sandwich bread. Bake at 375°F until bubbly.

Jamie Rawls

MAE'S MAXIMS

"Some use people and collect things. Others use things and collect people."

DESSERTS

Cakes

FRESH APPLE CAKE

1 c cooking oil
2 c sugar
2 eggs
3 c flour
1 tsp vanilla

1 tsp baking soda
1/2 tsp salt
1 tsp cinnamon
3 c chopped apples

Combine cooking oil and sugar. Add well-beaten eggs. Measure and sift together dry ingredients. Add dry ingredients to first mixture. Stir in apples. Bake in tube pan about 50 minutes at 300°F.

ICING

2 small pkg cream cheese
2 c powdered sugar

2 tbsp oleo
2 tbsp vanilla

Mix until smooth and spread on cake.

**Mae Winnon Mardis
& Jacque Winnon Burchfield**

APPLE DAPPLE CAKE

3 eggs
1 1/2 c vegetable oil
2 c sugar
2 tsp vanilla
1 1/2 c chopped pecans

3 c flour
1 tsp salt
1 tsp baking soda
3 c chopped baking apples

Topping

1 c brown sugar
1/4 c milk

1 stick butter or margarine

Preheat oven to 350°F. Mix eggs, oil, sugar, and vanilla, and blend well. Sift together flour, salt, and soda. Add flour to egg mixture and then apples and pecans. Pour into a greased tube pan, Bundt pan, or two loaf pans. Bake 1 hour and 20 minutes.

Topping: In saucepan, combine brown sugar, milk, and butter and cook 2 minutes. While cake is still hot, pour topping over the cake in the pan. Allow cake to cool completely before removing from the pan.

Jacque Winnon Burchfield

BANANA COCONUT CAKE

3/4 c shortening	1 tsp baking soda
1 1/2 c sugar	1 tsp baking powder
2 eggs	1/2 tsp salt
1 c ripe bananas, mashed	1/2 c buttermilk
1 tsp vanilla extract	1/2 c chopped pecans, optional
2 c cake flour	1 c flaked coconut

In a mixing bowl, cream shortening and sugar until fluffy. Add eggs; beat for 2 minutes. Add bananas and vanilla; beat for 2 minutes. Combine dry ingredients. Add the creamed mixture alternately with buttermilk. Mix well. Stir in pecans if desired. Pour into two greased and floured 9-inch cake pans. Sprinkle each with coconut. Bake at 375°F for 25–30 minutes or until cake test done; loosely cover with foil during the last 10 minutes of baking. Cool in pans 15 minutes before removing to a wire rack, coconut side up.

BUTTER-CREAM FROSTING

1/2 c shortening	pinch of salt
1/2 tsp vanilla extract	2 c confectioner's sugar
1/2 c butter or margarine, softened	1/4 c cold evaporated milk
1/2 tsp coconut extract	

In a mixing bowl, cream shortening and butter. Add remaining frosting ingredients. Mix on low until combined; beat on high for 5 minutes. Place one cake layer, coconut side down, on a cake plate; spread with some of the frosting. Top with second layer, coconut side up; frost sides and 1 inch around top edge of cake, leaving coconut center showing. Yield: 12 servings.

Ivy Gene Hamby Winnon

BLUEBERRY CAKE

Cook 1 Duncan Hines butter cake mix in 2 layers. Let cool.

ICING

1/2 c powdered sugar
1/2 c sugar
1 can blueberry pie filling

1 8-oz cream cheese
1 8-oz Cool Whip

Beat powdered sugar, sugar, and cream cheese until smooth. Fold in Cool Whip. Spread between layers, then spread half can blueberry pie filling on icing. Finish icing the top of cake and spread with remaining blueberry pie filling, letting it drip down the sides. Refrigerate leftovers.

Jacque Winnon Burchfield

BLUEBERRY DESSERT

1 angel food cake broken into small pieces
1 8-oz Cool Whip

1 carton whipping cream
1 can blueberry pie filling

Whip cream until fluffy. Mix cool whip and pour or stir into angel food cake bits. Add pie filling. Do not stir very hard; just cut or fold the filling in. Spoon into dessert dishes and serve.

Jacque Winnon Burchfield

BUTTER RUM CAKE

1 box butter cake mix

1/2 c cooking oil
1 c water
1 c pecans, chopped

1 small box instant vanilla pudding
4 eggs
1 tsp rum flavoring

Mix and put in tube pan. Bake 350°F for 45–50 minutes. Remove from oven and poke holes in cake. Let stand 5 minutes. Pour syrup over it. Let set in pan 30 minutes.

SYRUP

1 c sugar
1/2 c water

1 stick oleo
1 tsp rum flavoring

Bring all to a boil except flavoring. Boil until sugar and butter are melted. Remove from fire and add rum flavoring.

Jacque Winnon Burchfield

"Draw a circle, not a heart, around the one you love, because a heart can break but a circle goes on forever."

BUTTERFINGER DESSERT

1 angel food cake

2 cans sweetened condensed milk

5–6 Butterfingers (crushed)

1 large container Cool Whip

Mix condensed milk and Cool Whip together. Layer first angel food cake, then add Butterfingers, then Cool Whip mixture. Repeat layers and top with remaining Butterfinger. Refrigerate overnight.

Merri (Cissie) Winnon Rushing

CARAMEL CAKE

1 box yellow cake mix

2 1/2 c sugar

1 tsp vanilla

1 stick butter

1 small can evaporated milk

Mix cake mix as directed on box. Bake in 2 9-inch round pans.

When cake is baked and cooled, make Caramel Icing by melting butter in iron skillet. Add sugar and dissolve. Add milk, stirring fast so it doesn't crystalize. Cook to soft-ball stage. Add vanilla and spread on cake.

Melinda Mardis Bryan

CARROT CAKE

3 c grated carrots

1 1/2 c oil

2 c all-purpose flour

2 c sugar

4 eggs, beaten

2 tsp baking soda

1 tsp baking powder

1/2 tsp salt

1 tsp ground cinnamon

1 tsp vanilla flavoring

1/2–1 c pecans, chopped

Combine all ingredients; beat well. Pour into 3 greased and floured 9-inch cake pans or one 9x13-inch pan. Bake at 350°F for 25 minutes. This is a specialty of Melinda's and really, really good.

1 8-oz cream cheese

1/2 c butter

1 box powered sugar

1 tsp vanilla flavoring

1 tsp lemon flavoring

1 c coconut

1 c chopped pecans

Mix all ingredients and cream well. Spread over cool cake.

Melinda Mardis Bryan

COCONUT CAKE

1 pkg yellow cake mix
(I like Betty Crocker)

2 c sugar

1/4 c white Karo syrup

pinch of salt

2 c coconut

1/3 c water

3 egg whites (I put extra
yolks in cake)

pinch of cream of tartar

1 tsp vanilla

Bake cake mix according to directions on box and let cool.

ICING

Put the first 4 ingredients in a heavy boiler with a handle. Let this boil until it spins a long thread when you dip a spoon and hold about a foot over the boiler. While the mixture is boiling beat your egg whites in a large bowl, about a 4-quart size. Beat until real stiff. When the mixture gets ready, gradually pour into egg whites, beating all the time. Add vanilla and heat until real stiff. Cover the cake and put your coconut on the layers. This makes a lot of frosting.

Barbara Foster Oliver

COCONUT POUND CAKE

AUNT BEATTIE'S "SCRATCH CAKE"

Aunt Beattie Winnon would often be pulling one of these cakes out of the oven when we dropped by to drink coffee. She called it her "scratch cake." It gets better each day! My kids loved this cake!

2 sticks butter

1/2 c shortening

3 c sugar

5 eggs

1 tsp rum flavoring

1 tsp coconut flavoring

3 c flour

1/2 tsp salt

1/2 tsp baking powder

1 c milk

Cream butter and shortening, alternately adding sugar, eggs (one at a time), dry ingredients, and milk. Beat until creamy (about 4 minutes). Bake in greased and floured Bundt-cake pan for 2 hours at 300°F. Turn out while still warm, and glaze as follows:

GLAZE

1 c sugar   1 tsp almond extract.

1/2 c water

Let come to a boil, add almond extract, and brush on warm cake. Glaze keeps cake moist for days!

Terri Winnon

COCONUT–SOUR CREAM LAYER CAKE

One year just a few days before Christmas, a friend of mine had to undergo emergency surgery. I made this cake for her. She said she ate it all during the Christmas holidays and declares it saved her life. So it is really good, rich and healthy.

1 butter cake mix   1 16-oz carton sour cream

2 c sugar   1 12-oz pkg frozen coconut
                                   (thawed)

1 1/2 c Cool Whip

Prepare cake mix according to package directions, making 2 8-inch layers. When completely cool, split both layers. Combine sugar, sour cream, and coconut, blending well. Chill. Reserve 1 cup of sour cream mixture for frosting. Spread remainder between layers of cake. Combine reserved sour cream mixture with whipped topping. Blend until smooth. Spread on top and sides of cake. Seal cake in airtight container and refrigerate 3 days (if possible) before serving. Keep refrigerated until all is gone.

Mae Winnon Mardis

CREAM OF COCONUT CAKE

1 yellow or white cake mix   1 can condensed milk

1 can cream of coconut   1 can flaked coconut

1 c chopped pecans   1 12-oz Cool Whip

Mix cake mix according to directions on box. Pour into 13x9x2-inch pan. Bake and cool completely. Using the end of a spoon, poke holes in the cake. Mix cream of coconut and condensed milk together. Pour over cake and let run into holes. Spread on Cool Whip and sprinkle with pecans.

Jacque Winnon Burchfield

CRANBERRY COFFEE CAKE

1 stick butter
2 eggs
2 c flour
3/4 tsp baking soda
1 8-oz can whole cranberry sauce

1 tsp baking powder
1/2 tsp salt
1/2 pint sour cream
1 tsp almond extract
1 c granulated sugar

Cream butter and sugar until fluffy. Beat in eggs and extract. Combine flour, baking soda, baking powder, and salt. Add to creamed mixture alternately with sour cream. Spread half of the batter into a greased and floured 10-inch tube pan. Spread cranberry sauce over batter. Top with remaining batter. Bake at 350°F for 55–60 minutes or until lightly browned. Cool 10 minutes. Remove from pan.

TOPPING

1 tbsp butter, melted
1 c powdered sugar, sifted

1–2 tbsp warm water
1/2 tsp almond extract

Combine ingredients and drizzle over completely cooled cake.

Lillian Winnon Atkins

DUMP CAKE

1 can Cherry Pie filling
1 can crushed pineapple (do not drain)
1 box yellow cake mix
2 sticks melted margarine

1 can coconut
1 c chopped pecans

1/2 c brown sugar

Mix all ingredients in oblong pan and bake at 350°F for 45 minutes or until done.

Jacque Winnon Burchfield

FIG CAKE

2 c plain flour
1 tsp salt
1 c cooking oil
1 c chopped nuts
1 c fig preserves

1 tsp baking soda
1 1/2 c sugar
3 eggs
1 c buttermilk
1 tsp each vanilla, cinnamon, cloves, and nutmeg

Sift dry ingredients, add oil, and beat well. Add eggs and buttermilk gradually. Add figs, nuts, vanilla, and spices. Bake in 13x9-inch pan at 325°F for 45 minutes.

ICING

1 c sugar	1 stick oleo
1 tsp corn syrup	1 tsp vanilla
1/2 c buttermilk	1/2 tsp baking soda

Mix and boil 3 minutes, then pour over hot cake.

Donna Winnon Cox

FUNNEL CAKE

2 c plain flour	1/2 tsp salt
1 tsp baking powder	2 eggs
1 1/2 c milk	

Heat enough cooking oil to fry funnel cake in a deep fryer or skillet until very hot. Put batter into a funnel. Be sure to cover the spout with one finger while filling the funnel. Hold funnel over hot oil and release some of the batter in a circular motion, then a crisscrossing motion to form one funnel cake. The funnel batter will rise and expand so be really careful about how much batter you use. You will soon get a feel for how much it takes. Cook until light brown on both sides. Drain and sprinkle with powdered sugar and serve while still hot.

Ivy Gene Winnon

HONEY BUN CAKE

1 yellow cake mix	1/2 c margarine
4 eggs	1 tbsp cinnamon
3/4 c oil	1 c brown sugar
8 oz sour cream	1 c chopped pecans

Mix together cake mix, eggs, oil, and sour cream. Put into greased 9x13x2-inch baking pan. Mix the remaining ingredients together and swirl over cake batter. Bake at 325°F for 40 minutes. While still hot, add icing.

ICING

2 1/2 c powdered sugar	4 tbsp milk
1 tsp vanilla	

Mix and pour over cake while still hot

Jacque Winnon Burchfield

ICE BOX FRUIT CAKE

Recipe from Mrs. Willie Winnon.

1 1/2 c pecans, chopped fine	1 box graham crackers
1 lb raisins	2 small or 1 large bottle cherries
1 lb marshmallows	1 can coconut
1/2 pt whipping cream	1 c fig preserves

Put marshmallows in a double-boiler with about 3 tablespoons of the cream. Melt, stirring often. Whip the rest of the cream and add it to the melted marshmallows. Mix crackers crumbs, pecans, raisins, and coconut together good. Drain cherries and figs, chopped fine, and add to mixture. If you need the cherry juice, use it. Put mixture in cracker box lined with waxed paper or plastic wrap. Press well into cracker box. Wrap wax paper over it, sealing it off. Store in refrigerator until ready to use.

Ivy Gene Hamby Winnon

ICE BOX FRUIT CAKE

48 large marshmallows	1 c raisins
3 sticks margarine	6 slices candied pineapple
3 c pecans, chopped	1 lb red and green candied cherries
1 lb dates, chopped	1 box graham crackers, crushed

Melt margarine and marshmallows in top of double-boiler. Crush crackers. Chop other ingredients. Mix all together. Press into a loaf pan and chill. Slice. Eat. (Good!)

Jamie Winnon Rawls

ITALIAN CREAM CAKE

1 stick butter	1 c nuts, chopped fine
1/2 c shortening	2 c sugar
5 egg yolks, slightly beaten	1 c buttermilk
1 tsp baking soda	2 c flour
1 can coconut	

Cream together butter and shortening. Add egg yolks, soda, nuts, sugar, buttermilk, flour, and coconut. Beat 5 egg whites. Fold into batter. Pour into 3 greased and floured cake pans. Bake at 350°F. Frost with Cream Cheese Frosting.

CREAM CHEESE FROSTING

1 stick oleo

1 tsp vanilla

1 box confectioner's sugar

1 8-oz pkg cream cheese
(room temperature)

Blend all ingredients together. Finely chopped nuts may be added to the frosting.

**Lillian Winnon Atkins &
Jacque Winnon Burchfield**

JELL-O CAKE

1 box white cake mix

1 box Jell-O

3/4 c oil

3/4 c water

4 eggs

Mix Jell-O and cake mix dry, by hand. Add oil and water. Mix until smooth. Add eggs one at a time. Bake at 400°F in loaf or tube pan.

Lillian Winnon Atkins

KING CAKE

2 large cans crescent rolls

Filling

1 c powdered sugar

1 6-oz pkg cream cheese,
softened

2 tsp cinnamon

1 c finely chopped pecans

Icing

3 c powdered sugar

3 tbsp lemon juice

3 tbsp milk

1 tsp corn starch

Preheat oven to 350°F. Unroll crescent rolls (saving some to patch with) and place them overlapping on a baking sheet in a circle pattern with large side to the outside of pan and point towards the center.

Beat cream cheese, gradually adding powdered sugar and cinnamon until smooth. Spread cream cheese mixture in the center of crescent roll circle. Sprinkle with pecans, starting at the outside of ring. Bring ends towards the center. Then pull the inside of the dough to the center. Use any leftover crescent rolls to fill in gaps if needed.

Bake for 35 minutes or until lightly browned. When cooled, hide baby figurine in cake.

For icing, mix powdered sugar with milk and lemon juice. May have to adjust for desired consistency. Add vanilla and mix well. Divide icing into 3 bowls. Mix each with food coloring: yellow, green, and purple (red and blue make purple). Ice cake, alternating icing colors.

Jacque Winnon Burchfield

LEMON-BUNDT CAKE

1 yellow cake mix	4 eggs
1 can lemon icing	1 c water
1/2 c cooking oil	

Mix well and pour into a greased Bundt or tube pan. Bake at 350°F for approximately one hour. Check doneness after 45 minutes as oven temperatures vary. This can be done with any cake mix/icing combination. The original recipe called for a yellow cake mix and Coconut Pecan icing. My husband won't eat coconut, so I improvised with the lemon icing. He really likes this cake, especially when it first comes out of the oven . . . Yum!!

June Winnon Dawkins

OOGEE GOOEE CAKE

1 box yellow cake mix	1 stick oleo
1 egg	1 c chopped pecans

Mix these 4 ingredients together until crumbly. Spread into 13x9-inch pan. Then add topping mix.

TOPPING

1 8-oz pkg cream cheese	1 egg
1 box powdered sugar	

Mix these 3 ingredients all together. Spread on top of cake mixture. Bake at 350°F for 35–40 minutes, until golden brown. Let cake cool completely before cutting.

Melinda Mardis Bryan

POPPY SEED CAKE

2 c flour	1 c milk
1 tsp salt	1 tbsp poppy seeds
1 tsp baking powder	1 tsp vanilla
2 eggs	1 tsp butter extract
3/4 c oil	1 tsp almond extract
1 1/2 c sugar	

Mix all ingredients; beat 2 minutes with electric mixer. Pour in loaf pan. Bake 1 hour at 350°F.

TOPPING

¹/₄ c orange juice

¹/₂ c sugar

1 tsp almond extract

1 tsp vanilla

1 tsp butter extract

Mix together and pour over hot cake in pan. Let set 20 minutes and remove from pan.

Jacque Winnon Burchfield

PUNCH BOWL CAKE

1 box cake mix

1 large can crushed pineapple

2 boxes vanilla pudding and pie filling mix

1 can strawberry pie filling

1 large carton commercial pre-pared whipped topping

fresh strawberries for garnish

1 c chopped nuts

Cook cake mix according to box directions. When cake is done, crumble up into a punch bowl. While it is still hot, pour crushed pine-apple over top. Cool, then make up vanilla pudding and pie-filling mix according to package directions, and spread over top. Next, layer can of strawberry pie filling over all and spread whipped top-ping on top of this. Garnish with fresh strawberries.

Variations:

Peach filling with fresh peaches; cherry pie filling with cherries; or any of the above fillings and decorate with chopped nuts.

Ivy Gene Winnon

PINEAPPLE CAKE

1 box butter cake mix, baked as directed

1 egg yolk

1 ¹/₂ c sugar

1 large can crushed pineapple

1 tsp vanilla

¹/₄ c flour

Bake cake as directed on box. Filling: Cook last five ingredients until thick. Spread on cake. Makes a delicious cake and will keep for some time.

Ivy Gene Hamby Winnon

PINEAPPLE SKILLET CAKE

This recipe was given to me by my first mother-in-law, Nell Sims Caldwell.

1 c brown sugar   pineapple slices
3 tbsp butter   cherries

Melt sugar and butter in a 10-inch iron skillet. On top of this, arrange pineapple slices with cherries in holes.

CAKE

3 eggs, beaten slightly   1 1/2 c sifted flour
1 1/2 c white sugar   1 1/2 tsp baking powder
1/2 c cold water   1 tsp vanilla

Mix ingredients and pour into skillet, on top of mixture. Bake at 350°F for approximately 45 minutes. While still hot, place a large plate over skillet. Turn over so that the cake falls out of skillet onto plate.

June Winnon Dawkins

PINEAPPLE UPSIDE-DOWN CAKE

3 tbsp butter or margarine   1/2 c pineapple juice
2 c brown sugar   1 c flour
1 can sliced and drained   1 tsp baking powder
pineapple
2 eggs   1 tsp vanilla

Melt butter and 1 cup of the brown sugar in iron skillet. Place pineapple over this. Beat eggs, and add 1 cup of brown sugar, pineapple juice, flour, baking powder, and vanilla. Pour this cake mixture over the pineapple in the iron skillet. Bake in 350°F oven until straw comes out clean. Cool in skillet 10 minutes. Turn upside-down onto plate.

Jacque Winnon Burchfield

PINEAPPLE UPSIDE-DOWN CAKE

1/2 c butter   pineapple, drained
1/2 c brown sugar (packed)   pecans
cherries

Prepare Pan: Melt butter in heavy 10-inch skillet or 9-inch square pan. Sprinkle brown sugar evenly over butter. Arrange drained pineapple (crushed may be used if well drained) in attractive pattern on the butter-sugar coating. Decorate with pecan halves and cherries, if desired.

CAKE BATTER

1/2 c sifted flour	1/3 c soft shortening
2 tsp baking powder	1 tsp vanilla
1/2 tsp salt	2/3 c milk
1 c sugar	1/2 tsp lemon flavoring, if desired

1 egg

Sift together flour, baking powder, sugar, and salt. Then add shortening, vanilla, milk, and lemon flavoring. Add 1 egg. Beat 2 more minutes. Pour over fruit. Bake at 350°F for 40–45 minutes or until toothpick comes out clean. Immediately turn onto serving plate. Leave pan over cake a few minutes.

Mix in saucepan. Brown sugar and cornstarch. Stir in pineapple juice. Bring to boil for 1 minute. Add butter and lemon juice.

**Lillian Winnon Atkins
& Jacque Winnon Burchfield**

ORANGE-PINEAPPLE CAKE

1 box yellow cake mix	1 c oil
1 can mandarin oranges, undrained	4 eggs

Mix cake mix, oranges, oil, and eggs together. Beat at medium speed for 4 minutes. Pour into 3 greased and floured cake pans.* Bake at 350°F for 20–30 Minutes. Cool cake completely before frosting with following icing.

ICING

1 11-oz can crushed pineapple	1 9-oz Cool Whip
1 3-oz vanilla pudding mix	

Mix pineapple juice together with pudding mix and Cool Whip. Frost sides of layers of cake. Make sure cake is completely cooled.

*I cook mine in a 9x13 pan; it's easier than layers.

Ivy Gene Hamby Winnon

DELL'S HAWAIIAN CAKE

From Granny Warner

1 yellow cake mix	1 large instant vanilla pudding
1 8-oz cream cheese	2 c milk
1 8-oz Cool Whip	1 16-oz crushed pineapple
1 can angel flake coconut	

Bake cake according to directions. Let cool. Mix cream cheese, pudding, and milk; beat until thick. Pour over cake. Drain pineapple; spread over pudding mix. Add Cool Whip; then sprinkle coconut over Cool Whip.

Jacque Winnon Burchfield

7-UP PINEAPPLE CAKE

1 box yellow cake mix	1 1/3 c 7-Up
3/4 c oil	1 pkg vanilla pudding mix
4 eggs	

Combine all ingredients. Pour into 2 round cake pans. Bake at 350°F for 45 to 50 minutes. When done put together with icing.

ICING

1 1/2 c sugar	1 stick butter
2 eggs, beaten	1 small can crushed pineapple
3 tbsp flour	

Combine sugar, eggs, and flour in saucepan. Add pineapple and cook until thickened, stirring constantly. Spread on cake.

Melinda Mardis Bryan

ADELL'S DELUXE POUND CAKE

From Marie Crain

5 eggs	1 c sweet milk
2 sticks butter	1 tsp coconut flavoring
3 c flour, plain	1 tsp rum flavoring
1/2 c Crisco	3 c sugar
1/2 tsp salt	1/2 tsp baking powder

Let butter and Crisco come to room temperature. Cream with sugar until light and fluffy. Add eggs one at a time, beating 1 minute after each egg has been added. Add flavoring. Alternately add mixed dry ingredients and milk to the butter mixture—beginning and ending with flour. Use Angel Cake pan or large Bundt pan. Bake at 325°F about 1 1/2 hours.

Joan Winnon

AUNT VERA'S POUND CAKE

2 sticks butter	1/4 tsp soda
3 c sugar	1/2 tsp salt
1 c sour cream	3 c all-purpose flour
6 eggs	1 tsp vanilla

Cream together butter and sugar. Add eggs one at a time, beating after each one. Sift dry ingredients 3 times together. Add alternately with sour cream. Bake in a greased and floured tube pan at 350°F for 1 1/2 hours. Cool in pan for 30 minutes before removing.

Ivy Gene Hamby Winnon

MRS. PRICE POUND CAKE

I have no idea who Mrs. Price is—I got this recipe from someone else and claimed it because is the most delicious pound cake I had ever made.

1 lb Kraft Miracle whipped margarine

3 c sugar

3 c all-purpose flour

8 eggs

1 tsp vanilla

Have margarine and eggs at room temperature. Then mix well. Add other ingredients and mix well and bake at 300°F for 1 1/2 hours.

Mae Winnon Mardis

CARAMEL-NUT POUND CAKE

1 c butter

1/2 c shortening

1 1-lb pkg light brown sugar

1 c white sugar

5 eggs

1/2 tsp baking powder

1/2 tsp salt

3 c all-purpose flour

1 c milk

1 tbsp vanilla

1 c finely chopped nuts

Cream butter, shortening, and brown sugar thoroughly. Gradually add white sugar and continue creaming. Add eggs one at a time, beating thoroughly after each one. Combine baking powder, salt, and flour. Add alternately with milk to creamed mixture, beginning and ending with flour. Add vanilla and nuts. Blend well. Pour batter into well-greased and floured 10-inch tube pan. Bake at 325°F for 1 1/2 hours or until cake test done. Cool cake for 15 minutes before removing from pan.

Ivy Gene Winnon

EGGNOG-PECAN POUND CAKE

This is a good Christmas cake.

1 c butter softened (margarine will not be as good)

1/2 vegetable oil

3 c sugar

6 large eggs

3 c all purpose flour

1 tsp baking powder

1 1/2 c refrigerated eggnog

1 tsp vanilla

1 tsp butter flavor

2 c chopped pecans

Beat butter and vegetable oil at medium speed for 2 minutes. Add sugar and beat 5–7 minutes (or until sugar is mixed well). Add eggs, one at a time, and beat until yellow is mixed well. Combine dry ingredients to butter mixture, then add eggnog. Stir in vanilla and butter flavor. Fold in pecans. Pour into 10-inch tube pan or 2 loaf pans. Bake at 350°F for 1 hour 15 minutes. Cool in pan on wire rack 10–15 minutes. Remove from pan. Cool completely.

Jamie Rawls

SOUR CREAM–ALMOND POUND CAKE

1/2 lb butter	1/2 tsp baking soda
3 c flour	6 eggs
2 c sugar	1/2 tsp orange extract
1 8-oz sour cream	1/2 tsp almond extract

Cream butter and sugar. Add sour cream. Sift together flour and baking soda. Add to cream mix alternately with eggs. Add extract. Bake at 325°F for 1 hour 20 min.

Joan Winnon

PUMPKIN CRUMBLE

1 15-oz can pumpkin	1 tbsp pumpkin pie spice
1 12-oz can evaporated milk	1 yellow cake mix
3 eggs	3/4 c butter
1 c sugar	

Mix together the first 5 ingredients. Pour into a 9x13-inch cake pan. Sprinkle the dry yellow cake mix over top. Add pats of softened butter to top. Bake at 350°F for 1 hour and 10 minutes. Cool and cut into squares.

Joyce Atkins Keller

AMAZIN' RAISIN CAKE

3 c unsifted flour	1/2 tsp ground cinnamon
2 c sugar	1/2 tsp nutmeg
1 c mayonnaise	1/2 tsp salt
1/3 c milk	1/4 tsp ground cloves
2 eggs	3 c apples, chopped & peeled
2 tsp baking powder	1 c raisins
1/2 c chopped walnuts	

Grease and flour 2 9-inch round cake pans. In large bowl with mixer at low speed beat first 10 ingredients 2 minutes, scraping bowl frequently, or beat vigorously 300 strokes by hand. (Batter will be thick.) With spoon, stir in apples, raisins, and nuts. Spoon batter into pans. Bake in 350°F oven 45 minutes or until tester inserted in center comes out clean. Cool in pans 10 minutes. Remove, cool, fill and frost with 2 cups of whipped cream.

Ivy Gene Winnon

RED VELVET CAKE

1/2 c shortening	1 tsp vanilla
1 1/2 c sugar	3 tbsp cocoa
2 eggs	2 1/4 c flour
2 oz red food coloring (2 1-oz bottles)	1 tsp vinegar
1 c buttermilk	1 tsp baking soda
3/4 tsp salt	

Make paste with cocoa and red food coloring. Cream shortening with sugar. Add eggs; blend well. Add cocoa–food coloring mixture to creamed shortening–sugar–egg mixture. Combine sifted, measured flour with salt; add alternately with buttermilk and vanilla to creamed mixture. If using an electric mixer, remove mixer blades and fold in vinegar and soda. Pour batter in equal portions into three 8-inch layer-cake pans, greased and lined with wax paper. Bake at 350°F for 25–30 minutes.

ICING

The icing for this cake is just as unusual as the cake itself. One point is very important for its success. The first mixture must be thoroughly chilled before the second can be added to it. If it isn't it will curdle.

First Mixture:

3 tbsp flour	1 c milk

Add a little milk to flour, stirring until all lumps are gone. Add remaining milk. Cook, stirring constantly until thick. Cool. Chill in refrigerator until very cold.

Second Mixture:

1 c butter or margarine	1 c granulated sugar
1 tsp vanilla	

Bring butter to room temperature, add sugar, and cream until light and fluffy. If using mixer, beat 15–20 minutes, or until desired consistency. Add vanilla. Combine the two mixtures thoroughly. Spread rather thinly between layers. Use remaining icing to frost top and sides of cake.

**Jamie Winnon Rawls
& Jacque Winnon Burchfield**

SAD CAKE

4 eggs	1 can coconut
1 box brown sugar	2 c Bisquick
1 c chopped nuts	

Mix ingredients together. Bake at 350°F in 9x13-inch pan for 30 minutes.

Jacque Winnon Burchfield

SCRIPTURE CAKE

In loving memory of Mrs. Willie Winnon.

1 c Judges 5:25 (butter)	4 1/2 c 1 Kings 4:22 (flour)
2 c Jeremiah 6:20 (sugar)	1 tsp Amos 4:5 (baking powder)
2 tbsp Samuel 14:25 (honey)	1 c Samuel 30:12 (raisins)
6 Jeremiah 17:10 (eggs)	1 c Nahum 3:12 (figs)
1/2 c Judges 4:19 (milk)	2 Chronicles 9:9 (spice to taste)

Cream together butter, sugar, and honey (Luke 12:47). Beat eggs until frothy. Add milk to eggs and add to creamed mixture. Beat thoroughly. Sift flour with baking powder. Add to creamed mixture. Beat thoroughly. Sift flour with baking powder. Add to creamed mixture. Chop figs with raisins. Add spices and add all together. Bake at 375°F in Luke 12:28 (oven), about 30 minutes. 1. Corinthians 11:24 (break or cut if for Easter). Luke 9:13 (eat it) with Jeremiah 31:3 (love).

Lillian Winnon Atkins

7-UP CAKE

3 c sugar	3 c all-purpose flour
2 sticks oleo	7 oz 7-Up
5 eggs	1 tsp vanilla
1/2 c Crisco	

Cream together sugar, oleo, eggs, and Crisco. Mix well. Alternate flour with 7-Up. Cook 350°F for 1 hour 10 minutes.

Ivy Gene Winnon

SOCK-IT-TO-ME CAKE

1 pkg Duncan Hines Buttery Yellow Cake mix

3/4 c oil or butter

1/2 c sugar

4 eggs

8 oz sour cream

1 c pecans, chopped

3 tbsp brown sugar

1 tsp cinnamon

Cream oil and sugar. Add cake mix. Add eggs, one at a time. Beat. Add sour cream and nuts last. Pour half of batter in tube pan. Mix brown sugar with cinnamon. Sprinkle over first layer of batter. Pour other half of batter on top. Bake at 350°F for 50–60 minutes.

Lillian Winnon Atkins

SOUTHERN LANE CAKE

1/2 c butter, room temperature

1 c sugar

1/2 tsp vanilla extract

1 1/2 c plus 2 tbsp all-purpose flour

1 3/4 tsp baking powder

1/4 tsp salt

1/2 c milk

4 eggs

Lane Cake Frosting

6 egg yolks, lightly beaten

3/4 c + 2 tbsp sugar

1/4 tsp salt

6 tbsp butter

3/4 c each coarsely chopped pecans, raisins, cherries, shredded coconut

1 c whipping cream, whipped

1/4 c rye or bourbon whiskey (do not omit)

Beat butter until fluffy. Gradually beat in sugar. Add vanilla. Sift together flour, baking powder, and salt. Add flour mixture alternately with milk to butter mixture.

Beat egg whites until stiff. Fold whites into batter. Divide batter between two 9-inch buttered round pans lined with wax paper. Bake at 375°F for 15 minutes or until done. Remove from rack. Let stand 5 minutes. Invert onto racks. Remove paper. Cool. Frost.

Jacque Winnon Burchfield

STRAWBERRY CAKE

1 box white cake mix	4 eggs
1 small box strawberry Jell-O	4 c mashed strawberries, fresh or frozen
1 c oil	1 c chopped pecans
1/2 c milk	

Pre-heat oven to 350°F. Grease and flour pan (this does better cooked in oblong pan—layers seem to slide when they are frosted). In large bowl combine cake mix and Jell-O, With mixer at low speed, add oil and milk. With mixer at medium speed, add eggs, one at a time, beating after each. Blend in strawberries and pecans. Pour into pan and cook about 30 minutes or until toothpick comes out clean. Cool (remove or leave in pan). Frost with Strawberry Filling.

STRAWBERRY FILLING

1 box powdered sugar	1/2 c mashed strawberries
1 stick oleo	1/2 c chopped pecans

Cream sugar and softened butter. Add strawberries and pecans and mix well. Spread on cooled cake.

Mae Winnon Mardis

TWO-EGGS CAKE

1/2 c shortening	2 1/4 c flour
1 1/2 c sugar	2 1/2 tsp baking powder
1 tsp vanilla	1 tsp salt
2 eggs	1 c + 2 tbsp milk

Stir shortening to soften. Gradually add sugar and cream together until light and fluffy. Add vanilla. Add eggs, one at a time, beating well after each. Sift flour, baking powder, and salt together and gradually add to mixture until smooth. Bake at 350°F for 25 minutes.

Jacque Winnon Burchfield

WATERGATE CAKE

1 pkg cake mix	1/2 c oil
4 eggs	1 box pistachio pudding mix
1/2 c orange juice OR 1 c 7-Up	1/2 c water
1 tsp almond extract	

Dump all ingredients together and beat well with mixer. Pour half of batter into a Bundt pan and pour enough chocolate syrup into 1/4 of the batter to make as dark as you like. Pour in pan and bake at 350°F until cake springs back.

ICING

1 stick oleo

6 tbsp buttermilk

1 tsp vanilla

3 tbsp cocoa

1 lb powdered sugar

Bring to boil oleo, buttermilk, and cocoa. Add all of powdered sugar. Mix well. Add vanilla.

Lillian Winnon Atkins
& Jacque Winnon Burchfield

BUTTERFINGER CHOCOLATE CHIP CAKE

1 Swiss chocolate cake mix

1 box powdered sugar

1 8-oz pkg cream cheese

12 oz Cool Whip

1 Butterfinger Bar (crushed)

1/2 pkg semi-sweet chocolate chips

1/4 c water

Prepare cake as directed on box and divide evenly into 3 round cake pans. Bake until toothpick comes out clean. Cool. Mix sugar, cream cheese, Cool Whip until creamy. Spread on all 3 layers and around sides. Melt chocolate chips in water and mix well. Pour over top and let drizzle down sides of cake. Sprinkle Butterfinger pieces on top. Keep refrigerated until ready to serve.

Melinda Mardis Bryan

CHOCOLATE MAYONNAISE CAKE

2 c flour

1 c sugar

2 1/2 tbsp cocoa

2 tsp baking soda

1 c mayonnaise (Miracle Whip works just as well)

1 c water

1 tsp vanilla

Sift together dry ingredients. Add mayonnaise, water, and vanilla. Pour into 2 greased and floured cake pans. Bake at 375°F until cake springs back when touched in middle.

ICING

1 1/2 c sugar

1/2 stick butter

2 tbsp flour

1 small can Pet milk

Cook to soft-ball stage. Ice cake while still warm.

Ivy Gene Hamby Winnon

CHOCOLATE TOFFEE CAKE

1 box chocolate fudge cake mix	$1/2$ c vegetable oil
1 $1/3$ c water	3 eggs

Preheat oven to 350. Prepare cake mix, water, oil, and eggs. Pour into 3 8-inch pans greased and floured. Bake as directed on cake mix directions. Remove to wire rack to cool. Prepare frosting.

FROSTING

1 8-oz pkg cream cheese	$1/2$ c granulated sugar
1 c powdered sugar	1 8-oz package chocolate covered toffee bits
1 container frozen whipped topping, thawed	

Frost cake and refrigerate.

Jamie Rawls

FOUR-LAYER DELIGHT CAKE

MISSISSIPPI MUD CAKE

FIRST LAYER

1 stick oleo, room temperature	1 c chopped pecans
1 c flour	

Mix and press into 9x13-inch pan. Bake 15 minutes at 350°F. Cool.

SECOND LAYER

1 c powdered sugar	8 oz cream cheese
1 tsp vanilla	1 c Cool Whip

Mix. Sprinkle with $1/2$ cup of coconut. Pour over cooled crust.

THIRD LAYER

1 large box instant chocolate pudding	1 tsp vanilla
3 c milk	

Mix and spread over second layer. Refrigerate until firm.

FOURTH LAYER
Cover with Cool Whip. Sprinkle with nuts and coconut (optional). Refrigerate 1 hour.

Lillian Winnon Atkins
& Jacque Winnon Burchfield

GERMAN CHOCOLATE BUNDT CAKE

1 box German chocolate cake mix	4 eggs
1 can coconut-pecan frosting	2/3 c canola oil
1 c water	

Mix together well. Spray a Bundt-cake pan with Pam. Add the cake mix and bake at 350°F for 45–50 minutes.

10 Servings
Joan Winnon

HEAVENLY HASH CAKE

2 c all-purpose flour	1/2 pkg German sweet chocolate
2 c sugar	1 c water
2 sticks oleo (or butter)	1/2 c buttermilk
2 tbsp cocoa	1 tsp soda
2 eggs	

Mix soda and buttermilk; set aside. Sift flour and sugar together in a large bowl.

Place oleo, cocoa, chocolate, and water in saucepan; bring to rapid boil.

Pour over flour and sugar. Mix well.

Add buttermilk, soda, and eggs. Mix well. (Do not use mixer.) Pour into well greased and floured pan. Bake 25–30 minutes in 400°F oven.

ICING

1 stick oleo	1 box powdered sugar
1/2 pkg German sweet chocolate	1 tsp vanilla
2 tbsp cocoa	marshmallows
6 tbsp milk	pecans, chopped

Heat to boil, then add powdered sugar and vanilla. Beat with electric mixer. Cover hot cake with marshmallows and chopped pecans. Pour hot icing over marshmallows. Cool and cut into squares to serve.

> Note from Lillian: Instead of German chocolate, I use 4 tablespoons of cocoa, total, in cake, and 4 tablespoons cocoa in icing.

Jamie Winnon Rawls
& Lillian Winnon Atkins

CHOCOLATE FUDGE BARS

cooking spray

2 c firmly packed brown sugar

1 c butter, softened

1 tsp vanilla

1 large egg

2 7.4-oz pkgs Martha White chocolate chip muffin mix

1 1/2 c quick cooking oats

1 14-oz can condensed milk

1 12-oz pkg semi-sweet chocolate chips

1/2 c chopped walnuts (I used at least a cupful of pecans)

Heat oven to 350°F. Coat a 9x13x2-inch pan with cooking spray.

Beat brown sugar and butter in large bowl until light and fluffy. Beat in vanilla and egg. Stir in muffin mix and oats. Reserve one cup of this mixture.

Pat remaining mixture into prepared pan. Combine condensed milk and chocolate chips over low heat until chocolate is melted, stirring constantly.

Remove from heat and stir in nuts. Spread over muffin mixture to edge of pan. Drop reserved oat mixture by teaspoonful over chocolate mixture. Bake 35–40 minutes or until golden brown. Cool completely in pan.

I think these are to die for!

Marilyn S Winnon (Buddy)

HOT FUDGE PUDDING CAKE

1 1/4 c sugar, divided

1 c flour

7 tbsp Hershey's cocoa, divided

2 tsp baking powder

1/4 tsp salt

1/4 c milk

1/2 c butter, melted

1 1/2 tsp vanilla

1/2 c packed light brown sugar

1 1/4 c hot water

Heat oven to 350°F. In medium bowl combine 3/4 cups of sugar, flour, 3 tablespoons of cocoa, baking powder, and salt. Blend in milk, butter, and vanilla; beat until smooth. Pour batter into square pan—8-x8x2 or 9x9x2. In small bowl, combine 1/2 cup of sugar, brown sugar, and 4 tablespoons of cocoa; sprinkle mixture evenly over batter. Pour hot water over top; do not stir. Bake 40 minutes or until center is almost set. Let stand 15 minutes before serving.

Jacque Winnon Burchfield

MOLTEN LAVA CAKES

4 squares semi-sweet baking chocolate	2 eggs
1/2 c butter	2 egg yolks
1 c powdered sugar	6 tbsp flour

Butter 4 three-quarter-cup custard cups. Place on baking sheet. Microwave chocolate and butter in large bowl on high for 1 minute, or until butter is melted. Stir with a wire whisk until chocolate is completely melted. Stir in sugar until well blended. Whisk in eggs and egg yolks. Stir in flour. Divide butter between prepared custard cups.

Bake 13–14 minutes or until sides are firm but centers are soft. Let stand 1 minute. Carefully run a small knife around cakes to loosen. Invert cakes into dessert dishes. Serve immediately.

Connie Winnon Rowe

MOUNDS CAKE

1 chocolate cake mix	1 Eagle Brand milk
1 7-oz marshmallow creme	12 oz Cool Whip
14 oz coconut	

Cook cake as directed in 9x13-inch pan. Punch holes in cake and pour milk over it while hot. Cool. Combine coconut and marshmallow creme. Spread over cake. Refrigerate, then add the Cool Whip.

Joan Winnon

SHEATH CAKE

2 c all-purpose flour	1/2 pkg German sweet chocolate
2 c sugar	1 c water
2 sticks oleo	1/2 c buttermilk
2 tbsp cocoa	1 tsp baking soda
2 eggs	

Mix soda and buttermilk; set aside. Sift flour and sugar together in a large bowl. Place the oleo, cocoa, chocolate, and water in saucepan. Bring to rapid boil and pour over flour and sugar. Mix well. Add buttermilk, soda, and eggs. Mix well (do not use mixer). Pour into greased and floured pan. Bake 25–30 minutes in 400°F oven. I make this topped with marshmallows like Heavenly Hash cake.

ICING

1 stick oleo	2 tbsp cocoa
1/2 pkg German sweet chocolate	6 tbsp milk
1 box powdered sugar	1 tsp vanilla
1 c chopped nuts (optional)	

Heat oleo, cocoa, chocolate, and milk to boiling, then add powdered sugar and vanilla and beat with electric mixer. Spread on cake while hot. Add chopped nuts to icing, if desired.

Jamie Winnon Rawls

SHEATH CAKE

2 c flour	1 c water
2 c sugar	2 eggs
1 stick oleo	1/2 c buttermilk
1/2 c shortening	1 tsp baking soda
4 tbsp cocoa	1 tsp vanilla

Put flour and sugar in mixing bowl. Combine oleo, shortening, cocoa, and water in saucepan and bring to a boil. Remove from heat. Add chocolate mixture to flour mixture and beat until well mixed. Mix in eggs, buttermilk, soda, and vanilla. Bake at 350°F until done.

FROSTING

1 stick oleo	1 box powdered sugar
3 tbsp cocoa	1/2 c pecans
6 tbsp milk	1/2 c coconut

Put oleo, cocoa, and milk in saucepan and boil one minute. Add other ingredients and frost cake while warm.

Jacque Winnon Burchfield

TRIPLE-CHOCOLATE BUNDT CAKE

1 4-oz instant chocolate pudding mix	1³/₄ c milk
1 box devil's food cake mix	1 c chopped nuts
12 oz chocolate chips	2 eggs

Combine pudding mix, cake mix, chocolate chips, and nuts. Mix in very large bowl Add eggs and milk; mix by hand until well blended, about 2 minutes. Bake in greased and floured Bundt cake pan. Bake at 300–325°F for 55 minutes or until cake springs back from pan. Cool 30 minutes. Remove from pan and ice if desired.

Jacque Winnon Burchfield

TURTLE CAKE

1 box German chocolate cake mix	3 eggs
¹/₂ c oleo	1 can Eagle Brand milk
1 c oil	1 14-oz pkg caramels
1 c water	1 c chopped pecans

Cut oleo into cake mix. Add water, oil, eggs, and ¹/₂ can Eagle Brand milk; beat until well blended. Pour half of batter into greased and floured 9x13-inch pan. Bake at 350°F for 30 minutes. While cake is baking, melt caramels and ¹/₂ can Eagle Brand milk in double boiler or microwave. Stir in pecans; spread over hot cake. Add rest of batter and bake 30 minutes longer. Leave cake in pan.

FROSTING

2 c sugar	¹/₂ c cocoa
1 stick oleo	¹/₂ c Karo syrup
¹/₂ c milk	

Bring all ingredients to a boil; let boil for 2 minutes. Remove from heat and add 1 teaspoon of vanilla. Cool. Beat to spreading consistency. Spread over cake. Cut into squares.

**Jamie Winnon Rawls
& Jacque Winnon Burchfield**

BIRTHDAY CAKE FROSTING

¹/₂ c shortening	evaporated milk
¹/₂ c oleo	1 tsp vanilla
1 box powdered sugar	1 drop butter flavor

Beat shortening and oleo until fluffy. Gradually add powdered sugar, alternating with small amounts of evaporated milk until mixture is thick and fluffy. Add vanilla and flavor. Mix well. Tints any color.

Jamie Winnon Rawls

SEVEN-MINUTE FROSTING

This is the frosting I use on my coconut cake that I make from Duncan Hines butter cake mix.

2 egg whites

1 1/2 c sugar

1 tbsp white Karo

1/3 c water

Combine all ingredients in double-boiler. Mix up before placing over boiling water. Beat until mixture stands in stiff peaks (about 7 minutes). When peaked, fold in 1 teaspoon of vanilla. Will frost 2 or 3 layer cakes.

Mae Winnon Mardis

WHITE MOUNTAIN FROSTING

1/2 c sugar

1/2 c light corn syrup

1 tsp vanilla

2 tbsp water

2 egg whites

Mix in saucepan, sugar, corn syrup and water. Bring to rolling boil. Cook until syrup spins a 6–8-inch thread. Beat egg whites until stiff enough to hold a point. Pour hot syrup very slowly in a thin stream into the beaten egg whites. Beat until frosting holds peak. Add vanilla.

Lillian Winnon Atkins

FUDGE ICING

Given to me by Marilyn Gilbreth. I asked Marilyn if she would share this recipe, because every time we eat at church, she makes a flat cake and has this icing poured on top.

1 stick Parkay margarine

9 tbsp cocoa

4 oz evaporated milk

2 tsp vanilla

1 2-lb bag powdered sugar

The directions need to be followed exactly for this to turn out right.

Place margarine and cocoa in glass bowl. Microwave for 20 seconds. Stir well. Add 2 tsp vanilla. Stir well. Add small amount of powdered sugar. Stir well. Add a small amount of evaporated milk. Stir well. Microwave 20 seconds. Stir well. Repeat above steps until all the sugar and milk is used. I do this 7 times. Then I continue to microwave in 20-second increments until 4 minutes are up. Total cooking time is 4 minutes, but it takes approximately 20–25 minutes to get it made. When done, beat well and spread over cake.

Mae Winnon Mardis

Brownies, Cookies, etc.

BARRY'S BROWNIES

Barry learned to bake these when he was a very young kid, so he got to be very good and could get them just the right texture. Contributed by his Mom (Mae).

1 c sugar	1/2 c flour
2 eggs	1 tsp vanilla
6 tbsp cocoa	1/2 c chopped nuts
1/2 c margarine	

Add sugar to eggs and beat. Add softened margarine. Mix flour and cocoa and add to sugar mixture. Add vanilla and nuts.

Spread into a greased 8x8x2-inch pan. Bake at 350°F for 25 minutes. Do not overbake. Brownies need to be chewy.

Barry Mardis

BUTTERSCOTCH BROWNIES

1/2 c butter or shortening	2 tsp baking powder
2 c light brown sugar (packed)	1 tsp salt
2 eggs	1 tbsp vanilla
1 1/2 c sifted Gold Medal flour	1 c coarsely chopped walnuts or pecans

Melt butter or shortening over low heat. Remove from heat. Stir in brown sugar until blended. Cool. Stir in eggs. Sift together and stir in flour, baking powder, and salt. Stir in vanilla and chopped walnuts or pecans. Spread in well-greased 9x13-inch pan. Bake at 350°F for 25 minutes or until only a slight imprint remains when touched lightly with fingers. Don't over-bake. Cut into bars while still warm.

Kim Winnon AmRhein

CARAMEL BROWNIES

1 14-oz pkg light caramel candies	1/3 c evaporated milk
1/2 c evaporated milk (use a little less than 1/2 cup)	1 c chopped nuts
1 pkg Pillsbury German Chocolate cake mix	6 oz pkg chocolate chips
3/4 c melted margarine	

Over low heat melt caramels and scant 1/2 cup of milk. Set aside. Combine margarine, 1/3 cup of milk, cake mix, and nuts. Stir by hand until dough holds together. Press half dough mix into a 13x9-inch greased pan. Bake at 350°F for 5–6 minutes. Spread chocolate chips and melted caramels over the baked dough mixture, then crumble rest of dough over all. Bake 15–18 minutes in 350°F oven and when done remove and cool slightly. Refrigerate before cutting.

Jamie Winnon Rawls

Ruth's Brownies

A brownie mix (Betty Crocker Family size)	1 large Symphony large candy bar, milk chocolate
2 tsp water	1 large Symphony large candy bar, almond with toffee bits

Prepare brownie mix as directed but add an extra 2 tbsp water

Pour half of prepared mix into greased and floured pan. Break candy bars into individual squares, and alternate, a row of nuts and a row of plain candy bars, to cover mix. Pour the remaining mix over the candy.

Bake at 350°F for about 28 minutes. Do toothpick test but remember that the candy bars will be gummy. Cut with plastic knife.

Marilyn S Winnon (Buddy)

White Brownies

1 white cake mix	1/2 c brown sugar
2 eggs	1/2 c milk
1 pkg chocolate chips	1 tbsp corn syrup
1 c pecans	

Mix all ingredients together. Pour in 10x13-inch greased pan. Bake for 30–45 minutes at 350°F until golden brown.

Merri (Cissie) Winnon Rushing

Brownie Delight

1 family-size brownie mix	1 3.4-oz instant chocolate pudding
1 c pecans, chopped	toasted, chopped pecans (if desired)
1 8-oz cream cheese	chocolate sprinkles (if desired)
2 8-oz Cool Whip	

First layer: Spray a 9x13-inch pan with Pam. Bake brownies as direct-ed by box, adding 1 cup of pecans. Let this cool completely.

Second layer: Beat cream cheese until smooth. Fold in 1 tub of Cool Whip. Spread over the first layer.

Third layer: Mix pudding according to package directions. Let stand until set, 2–3 minutes. Spread on top of Cool Whip–cream cheese mixture. Refrigerate until set.

Fourth layer: Spread one tub of Cool Whip on top of chocolate pud-ding. Sprinkle with toasted pecans if desired or chocolate sprinkles. I let mine set overnight or may make early on the day to be served.

9 servings
Joan Winnon

TURTLE TRIFLE

low-fat brownie mix

fat-free Cool Whip

toffee candy bar or Nestlé candy bar

large box instant chocolate pudding

low-fat caramel sundae sauce

Bake brownies. Cool. Layer in trifle bowl: cubed brownies, sundae sauce, chocolate pudding, Cool Whip. Repeat layers, topping it with candy bar broken into pieces.

Gail Winnon Williams

TEA CAKES

2 sticks margarine, softened
2 eggs
1¹/₂ c sugar
2 tsp vanilla

¹/₂ tsp baking soda
1 tsp baking powder
3 c all-purpose flour

Preheat oven to 325°F Cream eggs, sugar, and margarine.

In separate bowl, mix dry ingredients. Blend dry ingredients with creamed mixture and let sit for a while. Mixture will be sticky. Drop by spoonfuls onto greased baking sheet. Bake until edges are brown.

Brenda Winnon Myers

LILLIAN'S TEA CAKES

3 eggs
¹/₂ tsp nutmeg (optional)
1 tsp vanilla
1 c milk

3 c sugar
3 or 4 c self-rising flour
1 c shortening

Sift flour into large bowl. Round out hole in middle of flour. Put in eggs, sugar, nutmeg, vanilla, and shortening. Mix with hands, adding milk slowly. Mix until dough is smooth. Then keep adding flour until you can handle dough with hands. Roll out to thickness of 1/4 inch. Cut out tea cakes. Bake in oven at 450°F for about 3–4 minutes.

Lillian Winnon Atkins

MAMA'S OLD TIMEY TEA CAKES

1/2 c butter	1 tsp vanilla
1 c sugar	1 tsp baking powder
2 eggs	1/2 tsp baking soda
1 tbsp buttermilk	plain flour, enough to make stiff dough

Mix dry ingredients thoroughly. Add butter, eggs, buttermilk, and vanilla. Roll out on floured board and cut with cookie cutter. Bake at 350°F until light brown—about 10 minutes.

Jesse Winnon

MAMAW BEA'S TEA CAKES

Mamaw Bea always made these for us and they were so good. Real good with a glass of cold milk.

2 sticks oleo	1 tbsp vanilla
1 1/2 c sugar	3 c flour
2 eggs	1 tsp baking powder
1/2 tsp baking soda	

Cream all ingredients, mix, and drop by teaspoon into a greased cookie sheet. Bake at 375°F until light brown. Cool and store.

**Rachel & Emerey Cox,
Ryeland Myers,
& Brenda Winnon Myers**

OLD FASHION TEA CAKES

2 c all-purpose flour	2 tsp baking powder
1 c sugar, plus 3 tbsp	1 c butter
2 eggs	1 tsp vanilla

Sift flour and baking powder together. Cream butter and sugar. Add eggs and mix well. Add flour and vanilla. Roll dough thin; cut with biscuit cutter. Bake 8–10 minutes at 400°F.

Jamie Winnon Rawls

LEMON TEA CAKES

1 1/2 c (3 sticks) margarine, softened

8 oz cream cheese, softened

2 1/4 c granulated sugar

5 eggs

3 tbsp lemon juice

2 tsp lemon extract

1 1/2 grated lemon peel

2 1/2 c plain flour

1 1/2 tsp baking powder

1/4 tsp salt

Heat oven to 325°F. Coat 12-cup muffin pans with nonstick cooking spray and set aside.

With mixer on medium speed, beat butter, cream cheese, and sugar in bowl until fluffy. Add eggs one at a time, beating well after each addition. Mix in lemon juice extract and lemon peel.

On low speed, beat in flour, baking powder, and salt. Fill each muffin cup with about 1/3 cup of batter for a total of 28.

Bake at 325°F for 23–25 minutes, or until toothpick inserted in the center comes out clean. Cool in pans on wire rack for 20 minutes. Remove cakes from pans to wire rack and cool completely.

GLAZE

2 1/2 c confectioner's sugar

3 c milk

1 3/4 tsp lemon extract

In medium-sized bowl, blend confectioner's sugar, milk, and lemon extract until smooth. Dip top of each cake in glaze. Place on waxed paper to dry.

Yield: 28 Servings
Jacque Winnon Burchfield

BOILED COOKIES

2 c sugar

1/2 c evaporated milk

2 tsp vanilla

1 stick oleo

4 tbsp cocoa

Boil all these ingredients together for 1 1/2 minutes. Remove from heat and add 1 1/2 cups oatmeal and 1/2 cup crunchy peanut butter. Drop by teaspoons on waxed paper. Let cool and eat.

Mae Winnon Mardis

DISHPAN COOKIES

2 c brown sugar

2 c white sugar

4 c flour

2 tsp baking soda

2 tsp vanilla

2 c cooking oil

4 eggs

1 tsp salt

1 1/2 c quick-cooking oats

4 c corn flakes

Cream together brown sugar, white sugar, vanilla, cooking oil, and eggs. Add in separate bowl flour, soda, and salt. Mix with other mixture and add oats and corn flakes. Bake at 350°F on ungreased cookie sheet. Makes a lot of cookies so be sure to mix them in a large pan.

Mae Winnon Mardis

FIG COOKIES

1 c shortening

1 1/2 c sugar

2 eggs

4 tbsp evaporated milk

1 tsp vanilla

1/2 tsp almond extract

3 c pecans, chopped
and toasted

1 pt jar fig preserves, chopped

3 1/2 c plain flour

1/2 tsp salt

1 tsp nutmeg

1 tsp cloves

2 tsp cinnamon

Mix ingredients in order listed. Stir in pecans. Drop from teaspoons onto greased cookie sheet. Bake at 350°F for 12–15 minutes.

Mae Winnon Mardis

LADY BIRD JOHNSON'S LACE COOKIES

From Doug's Kitchen. Easy and delicious!

1/2 c flour

1/4 c brown sugar, firmly packed

1/2 c coconut

1/4 c margarine

1/2 c corn syrup

1/2 tsp vanilla

Mix flour with coconut. Combine syrup, sugar and margarine in saucepan. Cook over medium heat until well blended. Remove from heat and stir in vanilla. Blend in flour mixture. Drop by teaspoonful 3–4 inches apart on ungreased cookie sheet. Bake at 325°F for 8–10 minutes.

Kim Winnon AmRhein

MAGIC COOKIE BARS

1/2 c oleo

1 1/2 c graham cracker crumbs

1 14-oz can condensed milk

1 6-oz pkg semi-sweet chips

1 1/3 c coconut (1 3 1/2-oz can)

1 c chopped pecans

Preheat oven to 350°F. In 13x9-inch pan, melt butter. Sprinkle crumbs over butter; pour condensed milk evenly over crumbs. Top evenly with remaining ingredients; press down gently. Bake 25–30 minutes or until lightly browned. Cool before cutting.

Jacque Winnon Burchfield

MRS. FIELD'S COOKIES

The urban legend goes that someone paid $250 dollars for the recipe, and sent it to everyone to get her money's worth. Probably a hoax, but the cookies are good.

2 c butter	5 c oatmeal
2 c sugar	1 tsp salt
2 c brown sugar	2 tsp baking powder
4 eggs	2 tsp baking soda
2 tsp vanilla	1 24-oz bag chocolate chips
4 c flour	1 8-oz Hershey bar, grated
3 c chopped nuts (any kind)	

Cream together butter and sugars. Add eggs and vanilla.

Place oatmeal into blender and blend into a powder.

Add flour, oatmeal, salt, baking powder, and baking soda to butter mixture. Add chocolate chips, chocolate bar, and nuts.

Roll into golf-ball sized cookies, and place 2 inches apart on ungreased cookie sheets. Bake at 375°F for 6 minutes.

Makes 112 cookies
Mae Winnon Mardis

MOLASSES COOKIES

8 c flour	4 tsp baking soda
1/4 tsp salt	1 tbsp ginger
1 tsp cinnamon	3 c molasses
1 c shortening	1/2 c butter
10 tbsp boiling water	granulated sugar

Mix all ingredients together. Roll into bars and place on greased cookie sheet. Sprinkle with sugar. Bake at 350°F for 10 minutes.

Lillian Winnon Atkins

PEANUT BUTTER COOKIES

1 c white sugar	1 18-oz jar crunchy peanut butter
1 c light Karo	3 1/2 c Special K cereal

Bring sugar and Karo to boil. Remove from heat. Stir in peanut butter and Special K. Drop on cookie sheet. If the sugar and Karo cooks the least bit long, the cookies will be too hard. These are good nourishing cookies for children.

Rachel Watson Waller
(Melinda's daughter)

PEANUT BUTTER COOKIES

These are very good and easy so eat and eat and eat.

1 c butter (2 sticks)	2 eggs
1 c brown sugar	1 tsp vanilla
1 c white sugar	3 c all-purpose flour
1 c peanut butter	1/2 tsp salt

Cream butter with sugar. Add peanut butter. Blend well. Add eggs and vanilla. Sift dry ingredients together. Slowly add to creamed mixture—mix well. Drop with teaspoon on cookie sheet—spaced well apart—then dip fork in water and very gently crisscross on cookie, mashing flat. Bake at 350°F about 10–12 minutes.

Makes about 8 or 9 dozen
Mae Winnon Mardis
& Jacque Winnon Burchfield

PEANUT BUTTER COOKIE BLOSSOMS

1/2 c peanut butter	1 tsp vanilla
1/2 c white sugar	1/2 tsp salt
1/2 c brown sugar	1 tsp baking soda
1 egg	1 3/4 c all-purpose flour
2 pkgs Hershey's kisses	

Cream the first four ingredients. Add egg and vanilla. Sift flour, soda, and salt, and combine with creamed mixture. Shape into balls and roll in white sugar. Bake at 375°F for 8 minutes. Press chocolate into center of cookie. Return to oven for 2–5 minutes.

Joyce Atkins Keller

SUGAR-FREE PEANUT BUTTER COOKIES

1 c peanut butter	1 egg
1 c Splenda	1 tbsp flour

Mix and cook at 350°F. Let set until cool.

Jacque Winnon Burchfield

POWDERED SUGAR ITALIAN SLICES

3 c all purpose flour

1 tsp baking soda

1 tsp baking powder

¹/₄ tsp salt

1 c (2 sticks) butter or margarine, slightly firm

1 c sugar

2 large eggs

¹/₃ c sour cream

1 tbsp vanilla flavoring

¹/₂ c powdered sugar, sifted

Heat oven to 350°F. Spray the cookie sheet with Pam or line with baking parchment.

In a large bowl, thoroughly whisk the flour, baking soda, baking powder, and salt. Set aside.

In the bowl of an electric mixer, mix the butter on medium-high speed until softened. Add the sugar and mix until lightened. Reduce the speed to medium and add the eggs, one at a time. Then blend in the sour cream and vanilla. Scrape down the sides of the bowl as needed.

On low speed add the flour mixture, mixing just until combined. The dough will be sticky. Spoon the dough onto the cookie sheet, forming two strips about 15 inches long and 2 ¹/₂ inches wide, placing the strips 3 inches apart. With floured hand reshape each strip of the dough into the correct measurement.

Bake on the lower shelf for 25 minutes. Reduce the oven temp to 300°F.

Using the large offset spatula, carefully transfer one of the loaves onto a cutting board. Using a serrated knife, cut the loaf into ¹/₂-inch thick slices.

Return to the oven for 10 minutes to bake, then turn the slices over and bake for another 5–8 minutes or until the cookies are lightly browned around the edges. Remove from the oven and when cool enough to handle, transfer the cookies to a cooking rack set over a sheet of wax paper. Place the powered sugar in a sifter and sprinkle the slices heavily on both sides.

Makes 40 cookies
Joan Winnon

SUGAR COOKIES

¹/₂ c oleo, softened

1 c sugar

2 eggs

1 tsp vanilla

¹/₂ tsp salt

1 tbsp milk

2 ¹/₄ c sifted flour

1 tsp baking powder

¹/₂ tsp baking soda

Mix all ingredients. Bake at 425°F for 8–12 minutes.

Jacque Winnon Burchfield

Pies & Cobblers

FRENCH APPLE PIE

1 unbaked 9-inch pie shell	2/3 c sugar
7 c sliced apples	1/2 tsp ground cinnamon
1 1/2 tbsp butter	

Place sliced apples in pie shell. Mix sugar and cinnamon; spread over apples. Dot with butter and spread with topping.

TOPPING

1 c flour	1/4 tsp cinnamon
1/2 c brown sugar	1/2 c butter

Combine flour, brown sugar, and cinnamon. Cut in butter until crumbly. Spread over pie until completely covered. This mixture is enough for 2 pies. Extra can be stored in refrigerator until ready to use.

Bake at 375°F for 50 minutes.

Mae Winnon Mardis

BLUEBERRY CREAM CHEESE PIE

pie crust, any kind you prefer	1 c sugar
sliced bananas	1 pkg (2 envelopes) Dream Whip
1 8-oz pkg cream cheese	blueberry pie filling

Prepare crust. Place one layer sliced bananas over crust. In mixer blend cream cheese and sugar. Make Dream Whip as directed on package. Add to cream cheese and sugar. Spread over bananas. Top with blueberry pie filling.

Makes 2 9-inch pies
Lillian Winnon Atkins

MAE'S MAXIMS

" No one cares about how much you know until they know how much you care."

DOLLY'S BUTTERMILK PIE

This recipe came from Bobby's Aunt Dolly Mardis Holcomb.

1 1/2 c sugar
1/2 c margarine
3 eggs

3 tbsp flour
1 tsp vanilla
1 c buttermilk

Beat together sugar, softened margarine, eggs, flour, vanilla, and buttermilk. Pour in unbaked pie shell and bake in 350°F oven. It's done when you insert a knife in top and it comes out clean.

Mae Winnon Mardis

BLUEBERRY PIE

4 c blueberries
1 c sugar
1/4 c all-purpose flour
1/4 tsp salt

1 1/2 tbsp lemon juice
2 tbsp butter
double piecrust

Mix sugar and flour well. Sprinkle lemon juice over berries. Cover with sugar and flour. Toss well. Let set until crust is prepared. Line pie plate with 1 crust. Spoon berries into pie shell. Dot with half of butter. Put top crust on berries (or lattice crust). Top with remaining butter. Bake at 350°F for 50–55 minutes.

Jamie Winnon Rawls

BANANA SPLIT DESSERT

CRUST

1 1/2 c flour
1 1/2 sticks plus 2 tbsp butter

2 tbsp sugar
3/4 c pecans

Mix all ingredients for crust well. Press in oblong baking dish. Bake for 20 minutes at 350°F. Let cool.

FILLING

1 tub whipped butter
2 egg whites

1 box powder sugar
2 tsp vanilla

Mix filling with electric mixer. Spread on cooled piecrust.

TOPPING

1 15-oz can crushed pineapple, drained

2 large bananas, sliced

Spread pineapple on top of filling mixture. Place sliced bananas over pineapple. Top with large container of Cool Whip.

Jamie Winnon Rawls

BANANA CARAMEL PIE

1 can sweetened condensed milk, label removed	1 cooked piecrust
3 bananas, sliced	whipped cream
1 Heath bar, crushed	

In a deep pan, place sweetened condensed milk. Add enough water to cover can. Bring to boil and then reduce heat to medium-low. Cook for 3 hours, adding water as needed to keep can covered. Cool can overnight (opening hot can is dangerous). Slice bananas into piecrust. Spread cooled, cooked sweetened condensed milk (which is now caramel) over bananas. Top with whipped cream. Sprinkle with Heath bar and refrigerate.

Joyce Atkins Keller

SOPAPILLA CHEESECAKE

This is the only cheesecake I make. My family loves it . . . don't need a spring-form pan either!

2 pkg Pillsbury Crescent Recipe Creations dough	1 1/2 c sugar
3 8-oz packages cream cheese, softened	1 tsp vanilla

Preheat oven to 350°F. Unroll 1 package crescent-roll dough into the bottom of a greased 9x13-inch pan. Drizzle some of the butter over the pastry and then sprinkle liberally with the sugar/cinnamon mixture. Also drizzle some of the honey over this layer.

Use a mixer to whip cream cheese, sugar, and vanilla.

Note: Here is where you can vary the overall taste of the cheesecake by adding orange zest or other flavors. I like adding eggs because it makes it even richer and helps bind it up when it bakes. Be creative with flavors.

Pour the cream cheese and sugar mixture onto the bottom layer of dough and spread evenly. It should be about a half-inch worth.

Sprinkle some more sugar and cinnamon on this layer.

Unroll another layer of the crescent dinner rolls and spread on top.

TOPPING

1/2 c butter, melted	2 tsp cinnamon
1/2 c sugar	1 jar honey

Drizzle with the remaining butter some more honey (as much or as little as you want), then sprinkle the remaining sugar/cinnamon mixture over the top. Be liberal with this. Here is where you can sprinkle on some nuts of some type (pecans, almonds, whatever).

Bake at 350°F for 35–45 minutes or until golden brown on top and fairly firm to the touch. You will have to keep an eye on it and adjust the time, more or less, until it just seems right.

Let cool and serve with crème fraiche or vanilla ice cream, and then watch your guests' eyes roll back in their heads and tears come to their eyes.

**Kimberly Winnon AmRhein
& Jacque Winnon Burchfield**

CHESS PIE

1/2 c margarine	1 unbaked pastry shell
5 eggs, well beaten	2 c sugar
1 tbsp all-purpose flour	1 c milk
1 tsp vanilla	1 tbsp yellow cornmeal
2 tbsp lemon juice	

Cream butter and sugar. Beat in flour and cornmeal. Add eggs, milk, vanilla, and lemon juice. Beat well. Pour into pastry shell. Bake at 350°F for 55–60 minutes or until knife comes clean.

Lillian Winnon Atkins

CHESS PIE

From my Granny Warner

2 c sugar	4 eggs
1 c oleo melted	2 tbsp corn meal
2 tbsp vinegar	

Mix well and pour into semi-baked crust. Bake at 300°F for 1 hour.

Jacque Winnon Burchfield

CHOCOLATE PIE

1 c sugar	2 c Pet milk
4 tbsp flour	4 tbsp margarine
3 tbsp cocoa	1 tsp vanilla extract
3 eggs, separated	

Mix sugar, flour, and cocoa. Mix well. Add milk, a small amount at a time, until all of the milk is added. Add butter. Cook over medium heat, stirring constantly until mixture thickens. Add vanilla. Pour into a 9-inch baked piecrust. Cool.

TOPPING

3 egg whites	1/2 tsp cream of tartar
pinch of salt	6 tbsp sugar

Mix egg whites, salt, and cream of tartar and beat on high speed until it forms a peak. Add 2 tablespoons of sugar per egg white. Continue to beat while adding sugar. Spread on pie. Bake 350°F until golden brown.

Joan Winnon

CHOCOLATE PIE

1 c sugar	1 tbsp butter
3 tbsp cornstarch	1 tsp vanilla
dash of salt	1 baked 9-in pastry shell
2 c milk	1/2 tsp cream of tartar
3 eggs, separated	1/4 c plus 2 tbsp sugar
1 square unsweetened chocolate	

Combine 1 cup of sugar, cornstarch, and salt in saucepan. Mix well. Combine milk and egg yolks; beat with a wire whisk 1–2 minutes or until frothy. Gradually stir into sugar mix, mixing well. Place over medium heat and stir constantly until thickened and bubbly. Remove from heat. Add chocolate, butter, and vanilla, stirring until chocolate and butter melt. Pour into pastry shell; set aside.

Beat egg whites until frothy: add cream of tartar, beating slightly. Gradually add sugar, 1 tablespoon at a time, beating until stiff peaks form. Spread meringue over filling, sealing to edge of pastry shell. Bake and 350°F for 10–12 minutes or until golden brown.

Donna Winnon Cox

JAMIE'S CHOCOLATE PIE

1 c sugar	5 tbsp self-rising flour
3 tbsp cocoa	3 eggs, separated and beaten
1 small can Carnation milk, add enough whole milk to make 2 c milk	

Mix sugar, cocoa and flour until well mixed. Add enough milk to make a paste, add beaten egg yolk, mix well. Then add all of milk. Cook over medium heat, stirring until thick. Add 2 tablespoons butter and 1 tsp vanilla. Remove from heat and beat well with spoon. Cool slightly before putting in a cooked pie shell.

PIE SHELL

1 1/3 c plain flour   5 tbsp cold water

1/2 c shortening

Cut together flour and shortening until mixture resembles cornmeal. Add cold water one spoon at a time until dough holds together. Roll large enough to fit 9-inch pie pan.

Jamie Winnon Rawls

IRON-SKILLET CHOCOLATE PIE

This recipe was given to me from my friend Lillian Holcomb Phillips, who is Bobby's cousin.

1 c sugar   1 c milk

2 heaping tbsp flour   1 tbsp oleo

1 heaping tbsp cocoa   1 tsp vanilla

2 eggs

Melt oleo in iron skillet. Mix dry ingredients and add to oleo in skillet. Beat egg yolks and add milk, mixing well. Then gradually add to mixture in skillet and cook until thickens. When thick pour into pre-cooked pie shell.

EGG WHITE TOPPING

1 heaping tbsp cornstarch   2 egg whites

2 tbsp sugar   3 tbsp sugar

1/2 c water   1 tsp vanilla

Mix first 3 ingredients and cook until thickens; set aside to cool.

Beat egg whites and sugar until stiff. Add vanilla, then gradually add the first mixture to egg whites while beating. Put on pie and brown.

Mae Winnon Mardis

FRIED CHOCOLATE PIES

canned biscuits   3/4 c sugar

2 tbsp cocoa   butter

Roll out biscuits (not layered) as flat and round as you can get them. Mix together cocoa and sugar. Place small amount on 1 side of flat biscuit then a pat of butter and fold over. Mash edges together with a fork. Fry in any kind of oil you like. It's best to roll all the biscuits, then prepare all pies for cooking. It doesn't take long for them to cook so don't let them burn.

Tip: As the butter melts when frying, it may ooze out, so lay pie in oil butter-side-up first, and when brown turn very carefully. As you remove pie from oil, place on paper towels folded side down so you won't lose your goodies.

Mae Winnon Mardis

CHOCOLATE DESSERT

CRUST

1 stick margarine   1 c flour
1 c chopped pecans

Mix, pat into deep 10-inch pie pan or 2 smaller round pie pans. Bake at 300–325°F for 20 minutes or until brown. Cool and chill in refrigerator.

FILLING FOR CHOCOLATE DESSERT

1 8-oz pkg cream cheese   2 4-oz pkg instant chocolate
                                 pudding or 1 pkg chocolate
                                 and 1 pkg vanilla pudding
1 c powdered sugar   3 c cold milk
1 c Cool Whip

Mix and spread over cooled crust. Combine pudding with milk. Mix until thick. Pour over cream cheese layer. Top with remaining Cool Whip. Chill before serving.

Merri (Cissie) Winnon Rushing

FRESH COCONUT PIE

From Granny Warner

1 stick butter   salt
5 eggs   2 tsp vanilla
3 c sugar   2 c coconut

Melt butter. Add the remaining ingredients. Pour into unbaked pie shells. Bake 5 minutes at 350°F. Reduce heat to 300°F and cook until set, about 45 minutes to 1 hour.

Makes 2 pies
Jacque Winnon Burchfield

"To the world you might be one person, but to one person you might be the world."

FRENCH COCONUT PIE

3 eggs, beaten
1 1/2 c sugar
1 c milk
1/2 c butter, melted
1 unbaked pie shell (9 inch)

1 tbsp all-purpose flour
1 tsp vanilla extract
1 tsp vinegar
1 c shredded coconut

In a mixing bowl, combine all ingredients except pie shell. Pour into pie shell and bake at 400°F for 10 minutes. Reduce heat to 325°F and bake 40 minutes or until top is golden and the center is almost set. When cool, store in refrigerator.

Yield: 8 servings
Ivy Gene Winnon

MRS. CECIL'S COCONUT CUSTARD PIE

3 egg yolks
1/2 c melted butter
1 c sugar
1 c evaporated milk

1 c shredded coconut
1 dash salt
1 tsp vanilla

Mix ingredients. Pour into an unbaked piecrust. Bake at 300°F until brown and pie does not jiggle when moved.

Joyce Atkins Keller

BASIC CREAM PIE

1 c sugar
2 tbsp flour
2 tbsp cornstarch
pinch salt

2 c milk
1/2 stick butter
3 eggs, separated
1 tsp vanilla

In double-boiler top sift together sugar, flour, cornstarch, and salt. Mix well. Mix in egg yolks and milk. Drop in butter. Place over boiling water and stir until thickened. Add vanilla and flavoring and:

For chocolate pie:
2 tbsp cocoa

For coconut pie:
3/4 c coconut

For lemon pie:
juice of 2 lemons

For banana pie:
2 sliced bananas

Bake pie shell at 350°F until brown. Allow to cool. Pour in cream mixture.

To make meringue: Beat egg whites until thick and fluffy. Add a pinch of cream of tartar and 1/3 cup of sugar. Beat until peaks form.

Joyce Atkins Keller

FRIED FRUIT PIES

DOUGH

1 tall can Carnation Milk	1 egg
2/3 c Crisco	4 tsp sugar
1 tbsp baking powder	4 c flour

Cut Crisco into flour. Add milk and egg. Work together well. Chill in refrigerator. Will keep 2 weeks. Pinch off piece the size of walnut & roll out.

FILLING

1 pkg dried apples, peaches, or apricots	1/2 tsp salt
2 1/2 c water	1 c sugar

Bring to boil. Cook for 30 minutes on simmer. Add sugar and stir until sugar dissolves. Add 1 heaping teaspoon of filling onto rolled-out dough. Pinch together sides with fork. Fry in deep oil on medium heat until pie browns on one side. Turn over and brown on other side. Drain on paper towels. Both dough and filling will come out even.

About 24 pies
Jamie Winnon Rawls

BEST-EVER LEMON PIE

1 baked 9-in pie shell	1/3 c lemon juice
1 1/4 c of sugar	3 egg yolks
6 tbsp cornstarch	1 1/2 tsp lemon extract
2 c water	2 tsp vinegar
3 tbsp butter	

Mix sugar and cornstarch together in the top of double-boiler. Add the two cups of water. Combine egg yolks with lemon juice and beat until well mixed. Add to the rest of the sugar mixture. Cook over boiling water until thick, about 25 minutes—this does away with the starchy taste. Now add the lemon extract, butter, and vinegar and stir thoroughly. Put mixture into deep 9-inch pie crust and let cool. Cover with meringue.

NEVER-FAIL MERINGUE

1 tbsp cornstarch	1/2 c boiling water
2 tbsp cold water	1 tsp vanilla
pinch of salt	

Blend cornstarch and cold water in saucepan. Add boiling water and cook, stirring until clear and thickened. Let stand until completely cold. With electric beater at high speed beat egg whites until foamy. Gradually add sugar and beat until stiff, but not dry. Turn mixer to low speed and add salt and vanilla. Gradually beat in cold cornstarch mixture. Turn mixer again to high, and beat well. Spread meringue over cooled pie filling. Bake at 350°F for 10 minutes or until top is lightly browned.

8 servings
Joan Winnon

LEMON MERINGUE PIE

Connie says this is her daddy's favorite pie. He said when his Mama made this pie, she made two of them—one for him and one for the rest of the family. (You all may believe she really did this but his brothers and sisters don't.) So Connie says she must have loved him a lot because, even though this pie is worth the wait, from start to finish it takes about two hours to make. So this is usually Jesse's birthday, Father's Day, and Christmas present from her.

PIE CRUST

1 1/4 c all-purpose flour	1/2 tsp salt
1/3 c shortening	4 tbsp cold water

DO NOT use store-bought pie crust. It absolutely ruins the pie! Mix flour and salt together. Cut in shortening until pieces are the size of small peas. Add water. Gently toss until all is moistened. Form dough into a ball. Roll out, forming a circle about 12 inches in diameter. DO NOT STRETCH DOUGH. Ease into 9-inch pie plate. Trim to 1/2 inch beyond edge of pie plate; fold under extra pastry. Flute edges. Prick pastry with fork and bake at 450°F for 10–12 minutes.

MICROWAVE LEMON PIE FILLING

1 1/2 c sugar

1/3 c cornstarch

1 1/2 c boiling water

3 egg yolks, slightly beaten*

1/3 c lemon juice

1 tbsp grated lemon peel

3 tbsp butter

*Save egg whites for use in meringue.

Mix sugar and cornstarch together in 1 1/2-quart bowl. Add boiling water and microwave on high for 2 minutes; stir with a wire whisk. Microwave on high for an additional 2 1/2 minutes. Whisk again. Gradually add some of hot mixture to beaten egg yolks. Then add to remaining hot mixture. Mix well. Microwave on high for 45 seconds. Stir in lemon juice, peel, and butter. Pour into baked piecrust. Cool.

MERINGUE

3 egg whites

1/4 tsp cream of tartar

6 tbsp sugar

Beat egg whites with cream of tartar on high with an electric mixer until stiff peaks form. Gradually add sugar 2 tablespoons at a time until egg whites are stiff and glossy. Immediately spread over pie, carefully sealing to edge of pastry to prevent shrinkage. Brown in a 400°F oven for about 10 minutes. Watch closely so it does not burn.

Connie L. Winnon-Rowe

LEMONADE PIE

This was a favorite pie at my house when my kids were growing up. The pink lemonade makes it look pretty.

1 can frozen lemonade
concentrate (pink if possible)

1 can condensed milk

1 small Cool Whip

1 graham cracker crust

Thaw lemonade and mix well with milk. Stir in Cool Whip. Be sure all ingredients are well mixed. Pour into crust and refrigerate. Ready to serve almost immediately.

Mae Winnon Mardis

MILLIONAIRE PIE

2 c powdered sugar

1 stick oleo, softened

1 egg

1/4 tsp salt

2 baked piecrusts

1/2 tsp vanilla

2 pkg Dream Whip

1 c pecans

1 can pineapple, drained

Cream together the powdered sugar and oleo. Add eggs, salt, and vanilla. Mix well until light and fluffy. Spread on piecrust and chill. Whip cream until stiff. Blend in pineapple and pecans. Spoon into the pie shells and chill until ready to serve.

Jacque Winnon Burchfield

PEACH COBBLER

From Mamaw Beatrice Hamby

1 c sugar

1/2 c self-rising flour

1 large can peaches with juice

1/2 stick butter

Mix sugar and flour together. Melt butter in dish. Add peaches with juice to sugar and flour mixture. Add peach mixture to melted butter. Add water for desired consistency. Bake at 425°F until crust is golden brown.

Donna Winnon Cox

QUICK PEACH COBBLER

1 c sugar

1 c flour

1/2 tsp salt

1/2 tsp vanilla

1 stick melted butter

1/2 tsp baking powder

1 c milk

1 can peaches

Melt butter in 10x13-inch pan. Mix all ingredients together except peaches. Pour mixture in pan and add the can of peaches to top evenly. Bake at 400°F until golden brown.

Merri (Cissie) Winnon Rushing

PEANUT BUTTER PIE

4 oz cream cheese

1 c powdered sugar

1 graham cracker crust

1/2 c peanut butter

1 large tub whipped topping

Mix cream cheese, powdered sugar, peanut butter, and large whipped topping together. Fill pie crust and refrigerate to cool and serve.

8 servings
Joan Winnon

BAKED PINEAPPLE

1 large can pineapple chunks

1 c cheddar cheese

2/3 c sugar

1 1/2 c Ritz crackers, crumbled

3 tbsp flour

1/2 c melted butter

Drain pineapple (keep juice). Add sugar and flour to pineapple juice and cook to dissolve. Layer pineapple in baking dish. Pour juice over pineapple. Add cheese, then cracker crumbs. Drizzle melted butter over mixture. Bake at 350°F for 25–30 minutes.

Jamie Winnon Rawls

SOUTHERN PECAN PIE

1 c Karo syrup	3 eggs, slightly beaten
1 c sugar	3 tbsp oleo, melted
1 tsp vanilla	1/8 tsp salt
1 c pecans	1 9-inch pie shell, unbaked

Melt butter. Beat eggs. Mix together sugar, syrup, and eggs. Add butter, vanilla, and pecans. Bake on center rack at 350°F for 50 minutes to 1 hour.

**Lillian Winnon Atkins,
Jamie Winnon Rawls, Ivy Gene
Hamby Winnon
& Jacque Winnon Burchfield**

BOURBON-CHOCOLATE-PECAN PIE

1 refrigerated pie crust	3 tbsp bourbon*
4 large eggs	1 tbsp all-purpose flour
1 c light corn syrup	1 tbsp vanilla extract
6 tbsp butter or margarine, melted	1 c coarsely chopped pecans
1/2 c granulated sugar	1 c (6-oz pkg) semi-sweet chocolate morsels
1/4 c firmly packed light brown sugar	

Fit pie crust into a 9-inch pieplate according to package directions. Fold edges under and crimp.

Whisk together eggs, light corn syrup, and next 6 ingredients in a large bowl until mixture is smooth. Stir in chopped pecans and morsels. Pour into pie crust.

Bake on lowest oven rack at 350°F for 1 hour or until set. Makes 1 9-inch pie.

*Substitute 2 tbsp butter or margarine, melted, if desired.

Jacque Winnon Burchfield

Georgia Pecan Pie

2 graham cracker crusts

8 oz cream cheese, softened at room temp

8 oz Cool Whip

1/2 c powdered sugar

2 c chopped pecans

1 c coconut

1 stick butter

1 11.75-oz jar caramel ice cream topping

Melt butter in oven, then put pecans and coconut in butter and toast in the oven for 15 minutes, stirring every 5 minutes to keep from burning. Let this cool.

Mix cream cheese, powdered sugar, and Cool Whip with mixer until smooth. Spread half into each crust. Sprinkle pecan mixture evenly on top. Drizzle caramel on top of each pie. Refrigerate for 2 hours before serving.

Makes 2 pies
Mae Winnon Mardis

Pecan Delight

20–22 Ritz crackers, crushed

1 c sugar

1 c broken pecans

3 egg whites, beaten stiff

Mix dry ingredients thoroughly. Fold in egg whites. Pour in greased pie plate. Bake 20–25 minutes. Cool completely and top with whipped cream.

Lillian Winnon Atkins

Pecan Tassies

1 3-oz pkg cream cheese

1/4 lb margarine

1 c flour

pinch salt

Cream margarine and cheese until well blended, add sifted flour and salt; mix well. Let stand one hour while making filling.

Filling

1 c ground pecans

1 c brown sugar

1 tsp vanilla

2 eggs

2 tbsp margarine

Cream margarine; add sugar, eggs, nuts and vanilla. Blend well. Take small balls of dough and work into a small muffin tin to form a well. Using a teaspoon, fill each shell with filling, about half full. Bake at 325°F for 25 minutes. Cool 5 minutes before removing from tins.

Makes 3 dozen
Jamie Winnon Rawls

STRAWBERRY PIE

3 whole eggs, slightly beaten
3 tbsp cornstarch
1 c water

dash of salt
1 pkg strawberry Jell-O
1 pt strawberries, sliced

Cook over low heat, stirring constantly until thick. Then add Jell-O. Let cool to room temperature by placing pot in cool water. In pie shell, place sliced strawberries, then pour in Jell-O mixture. Chill and top with your favorite topping.

Mae Winnon Mardis

NO-BAKE SWEET POTATO PIE

2 env Dream Whip
1/2 tsp cinnamon
1 c cooked sweet potatoes or pumpkin
1 pkg instant vanilla pudding mix

1/2 tsp nutmeg
2/3 c milk
1/2 tsp ginger
2 pie shells, cooked

Prepare Dream Whip according to package directions. Add 1 cup of Dream Whip to pie and reserve remainder for top. Combine all ingredients. Mix well and pour into cooked pie shells.

Lillian Winnon Atkins

Custards & Puddings

EGG CUSTARD

This recipe came from an older friend at my church and it is really good.

4 eggs
1/3 c sugar
1/2 tsp salt

1 tsp vanilla
1 large can evaporated milk
1 c water

Beat eggs. Add sugar, salt, and vanilla. Mix well. Add milk (undiluted) and water. Sprinkle with nutmeg if desired. Pour mixture in 9-Inch unbaked pie shell (be sure you use 9 in or it will be to small). Bake at 425°F for 15 minutes. Lower temperature to 350°F and bake about 30 minutes or until inserted knife comes out clean.

Mae Winnon Mardis

OLD FASHION BANANA PUDDING

1 c sugar

3 tbsp flour

4 eggs

2 1/2 c milk (1 small can evaporated milk, the rest whole milk)

1 tsp vanilla flavoring

5 or 6 bananas

1 box vanilla wafers

Mix sugar and flour in top of double boiler. Add 1 whole egg and 3 yolks. Mix well. Stir in milk and cook until thickened. Remove from heat, add vanilla, and cool. Layer vanilla wafers, bananas, and sauce until all are used.

MERINGUE

3 egg whites

1/4 c sugar

Beat egg whites until stiff. Add sugar and beat until peaked. Cover pudding and bake in 425°F oven 5 minutes until brown.

**Jamie Winnon Rawls
& Jacque Winnon Rawls**

WHITE CHOCOLATE BREAD PUDDING

5–6 eggs, beaten

2 c sugar

1 tsp nutmeg

1 tsp apple pie spice

1/2 c butter, melted

1 bar white chocolate, melted

1 qt half and half

5–6 c cubed sourdough bread

1 c raisins

1 c chopped pecans

Combine first seven ingredients and mix well. Pour over sourdough bread, and add raisins and pecans. Refrigerate overnight, or at least 6 hours. Bake 350°F for 1 hour.

WHITE CHOCOLATE SAUCE

1/2 c sugar

3 tbsp flour, mixed well

1 egg yolk

1 1/2 c half and half milk

4 tbsp butter, melted

1 bar white chocolate

1 tsp vanilla

Mix sugar and flour. Add eggs and half and half. Mix well. Add butter and chocolate. Cook on medium heat until mixture begins to thicken and is smooth. Add vanilla. Serve over Bread Pudding.

Jamie Rawls

BETTY BOO'S CREOLE BREAD PUDDING

1 large French bread

1 small French bread

1/2 gallon milk

2 cans evaporated milk

2 c sugar

6 eggs

3 sticks butter, softened

1 large can crushed pineapple

1/2 jar cherries, cut in pieces

2 tsp cherry juice

1 c raisins

1 tsp each of vanilla, butternut extract, almond extract, pineapple extract, banana extract, lemon extract

Use a pan that is approximately 10x15x3. Preheat oven to 350°F. Cut French bread in 1/2-inch slices. Put in pan and pour evaporated milk and almost all of the 1/2 gallon of milk over bread to soak. Set aside.

Cream softened butter. Add sugar, a little at a time. Add eggs, one at a time. Beat until creamy. Add flavorings and beat well.

Add cherries, pineapples, raisins, and cherry juice to bread mixture. Add butter mixture and to bread and mix well.

Place in preheated oven for about 1 hour or until firm. Remove from heat and add whiskey or rum sauce (recipe below).

WHISKEY OR RUM SAUCE

2 sticks butter

2 c sugar

2 eggs

1/4 c rum or whiskey

In saucepan, caramelize butter and sugar until thick and creamy. Beat eggs and add to butter mixture. Beat quickly so eggs don't curdle. Remove from heat and add liquor. Pour over bread pudding.

Serves 20
Jacque Winnon Burchfield

ART'S BREAD PUDDING WITH VANILLA SAUCE

3 large eggs, lightly beaten

1 1/2 c sugar

2 tbsp light brown sugar

1/2 tsp ground nutmeg

2 1/2 c whipping cream

1/4 c butter, melted

4 c French bread, cubed

3/4 c raisins

Combine first four ingredients; stir in whipping cream and butter. Gently stir in bread cubes and raisins. Pour into a lightly greased 2-quart soufflé or deep baking dish.

Bake uncovered at 375°F for 50–55 minutes, shielding with foil after 30 minutes to prevent excessive browning. Let stand 10 minutes before serving. Serve warm with vanilla sauce.

Vanilla Sauce

1/2 c sugar	dash ground nutmeg
3 tbsp light brown sugar	1 1/4 c whipping cream
1 tbsp all purpose flour	2 tbsp butter, softened
1 large egg	1 tbsp vanilla

Whisk together first seven ingredients in a heavy saucepan; cook over medium heat, whisking constantly, 10–12 minutes or until thickened. Remove from heat; stir in vanilla. Serve warm or at room temperature.

Yield: 6–8 servings
Marilyn S Winnon (Buddy)

Miscellaneous

APPLE BROWN BETTY

Comfort food at its best!

2 c sliced, peeled, cored baking apples (about 4 medium apples)	1/4 c water

Crumb Mixture

3/4 c brown sugar (packed)	3/4 tsp cinnamon
1 c graham cracker crumbs	3/4 tsp nutmeg
1/3 c soft butter	

Blend the crumb mixture until crumbly.

Alternate layers of the sliced apples and crumb mixture in a greased 8-inch square pan. Pour 1/4 cup water over the top. Bake until apples are tender and topping is golden brown. Serve warm with ice cream.

Terri Winnon

APPLE ENCHILADAS

1 21-oz can apple pie filling
1 8-oz pkg flour tortillas
1 tsp ground cinnamon
1/3 c margarine

1/2 c sugar
1/2 c firmly packed brown sugar
1/2 c water

Spoon pie filling into center of tortillas. Sprinkle with cinnamon. Roll up and place seam side down in a lightly greased 2-quart baking dish. Bring margarine and next 3 ingredients to a boil in medium saucepan and simmer, stirring 3 minutes. Pour over enchiladas. Let stand 30 minutes. Bake at 350°F for 20 minutes. (Be sure to coat and cover with sauce.)

Gail Winnon Williams

DEATH BY CHOCOLATE

1 large bag of Oreo cookies
14-oz bag of caramels
5 oz condensed milk
1/2 c margarine

8 oz cream cheese
1 c powdered sugar
8 oz Cool Whip
1/2 c pecans, chopped

Crush 25 cookies and cover bottom of 9x13x2-inch baking dish. Combine caramels, condensed milk, and margarine, and melt over medium heat. Pour mixture over cookies. Cool in refrigerator. Mix cream cheese, powdered sugar, and Cool Whip. Spread over caramel mixture. Crush 12 Oreo cookies. Sprinkle cookies and pecans on top. Refrigerate 3 hours.

Jacque Winnon Burchfield

MAE'S MAXIMS

"Some people come into our lives
and quietly go—others stay awhile
and leave footprints on our heart
and we are never the same."

PINEAPPLE DUMPLINGS

CRUST

1/2 c water	1/2 tsp salt
1/2 c shortening	1 1/2 c flour

Make into a soft dough and roll out thin as for pie crust.

SPRINKLE

1/2 c sugar	1 #2 can crushed pineapple, drained (save juice)
1/2 c butter	

Roll up and slice into 1 1/2-inch slices. Place in baking dish.

JUICE

2/3 c sugar	pineapple juice
1/2 c water	

Pour over dough. Bake at 300°F for 30 minutes.

Jacque Winnon Burchfield

MAE'S MISC

How to Knit a Scarf

* Size 13 needles
* 1 skein of yarn

Cast on 15 stitches and knit every row until yarn is gone.

HARD CINNAMON CANDY

2 c sugar
1 c water
1/2 tsp red food coloring

1/2 c light corn syrup
1/4–1/2 tsp cinnamon oil*

In a large, heavy saucepan, combine sugar, water, and corn syrup. Bring to a boil over medium heat, stirring occasionally. Cover and cook for 3 minutes. Uncover and cook over medium-high heat, without stirring, until a candy thermometer reads 310°F (hard-crack stage). Remove from the heat; stir in oil and food coloring keeping face away from the mixture as the odor will be very strong.

Immediately pour onto a greased baking sheet. Quickly spread into a 13x9-inch rectangle. Using a sharp knife, score into 1-inch squares. Re-cut rectangle along scored lines until candy is cut into squares. Let stand at room temperature until dry. Separate into squares, using a knife if necessary.

*Cinnamon oil can be found in some pharmacies or at kitchen and cake decorating supply stores.

Yield: 1 pound
Jacque Winnon Burchfield

COCONUT BALLS

MARTHA WASHINGTON BALLS

2 boxes powdered sugar
1 can condensed milk
2 stick oleo
2 pkg coconut

2 c pecans, chopped
3 6-oz pkg chocolate chips
3/4 box paraffin wax

Roll out in small balls size of quarter. Place on cookie sheet and chill. Wet hands several times while rolling balls. Melt in top of double-boiler chocolate chips, paraffin wax, and 1/2 stick oleo. Use sharp sticks or toothpicks to dip balls into hot mixture and drop on wax paper. Cool.

**Lillian Winnon Atkins,
Jacque Winnon Burchfield
& Donna Winnon Cox**

DIVINITY CANDY

2 2/3 c sugar

2/3 c cold water

1 tsp vanilla

2/3 c white corn syrup

2 egg whites, room temperature

1 c chopped nuts

Mix together sugar, corn syrup, and water. Stir well. Allow to boil without stirring until it forms a hard ball in cold water. Pour this over stiffly beaten egg whites, beating constantly. Cool. Add vanilla and nuts. Beat until cool and thick enough to set. Pour onto buttered platter and cut when cool.

Lillian Winnon Atkins
& Jacque Winnon Burchfield

MARSHMALLOW CREAM DIVINITY

2 c sugar

1/2 c water

1/2 c nuts

pinch of salt

1 7-oz jar marshmallow cream

Combine water, sugar and salt. Bring to a rolling boil and boil only 2 minutes. (I take it to a soft-ball stage.) Put marshmallow cream into a large bowl and pour hot mixture all at once into it. Stir until candy loses it gloss. Add nuts. Drop by spoonfuls onto waxed paper.

Never fails unless you use too much marshmallow cream.

Marilyn S Winnon (Buddy)

MAMA'S FUDGE

2 1/4 c sugar

3/4 c Pet milk

16 large marshmallows or 1 jar of marshmallow cream

1/4 c margarine

1/4 tsp salt

1 c (6 oz) semi-sweet chocolate chips (I use milk chocolate chips)

1 c pecan pieces

1 tsp vanilla

Butter an 8-inch square pan (or line pan with aluminum foil and spray foil with Pam). Set aside.

Mix in a heavy 2-quart saucepan, sugar, Pet milk, marshmallows, margarine, and salt.

Cook, stirring constantly over medium heat to a bubbling boil (be careful . . . mixture might bubble over top of pan). Boil and stir for five minutes. Remove from heat.

Stir in chocolate chips until completely melted. Stir in pecans and vanilla. Spread in buttered pan and cool.

Cut into 30 pieces.

June Winnon Dawkins

FOUR-CHIP FUDGE

Easy!

1 ½ tsp + ¾ c butter, divided

1 14-oz can sweetened condensed milk

3 tbsp milk

1 12-oz pkg semisweet chocolate chips

1 11.5-oz pkg milk chocolate chips

1 10-oz pkg peanut butter chips

1 c butterscotch chips

1 jar marshmallow creme

½ tsp almond extract

½ tsp vanilla extract

1 c chopped walnuts

Line a 13x9-inch pan with foil and grease the foil with 1 ½ teaspoons of butter; set aside. In a large, heavy saucepan, melt the remaining butter over low heat. Add the next 5 ingredients. Cook and stir constantly until smooth. Remove from the heat; stir in the butterscotch chips, marshmallow cream, and extracts until well blended. Stir in nuts.

Spread into prepared pan. Refrigerate until set. Lift out of pan and remove foil. Cut into squares.

Yields about 4 ½ pounds
Connie Winnon Rowe

FIVE POUNDS OF FUDGE

2 12-oz pkg semi-sweet chocolate pieces

1 c margarine

1 7-oz jar marshmallow cream

4 ½ c sugar

1 12-oz can evaporated milk

2 tbsp vanilla

1 ½ c chopped pecans

Combine first 3 ingredients in a large bowl; set aside. Combine sugar and milk in buttered Dutch oven. Cook over medium heat, stirring constantly, until it reaches soft-ball stage. Pour over chocolate mixture. Beat at high speed until it thickens and begins to lose its gloss. Stir in vanilla and pecans. Spread in buttered long pan. Chill until firm.

Yield: 5 pounds
Mae Winnon Mardis

COCOA FUDGE

²/₃ c Hershey's cocoa

3 c sugar

¹/₈ tsp salt

1 ¹/₂ c milk

¹/₄ c butter or margarine

1 tsp vanilla

Thoroughly combine cocoa, sugar, and salt in a 4-quart saucepan; gradually add milk. Bring to a "bubbly" boil on medium heat, stirring constantly. Continue to boil, while stirring, to 234°F (be sure that bulb of candy thermometer is not resting on bottom of saucepan)—or until a small amount of mixture forms a soft ball when dropped into cold water. Remove saucepan from heat; add butter or margarine and vanilla. DO NOT STIR. Cool at room temperature to 110°F. Beat by hand until fudge thickens and loses some of its gloss. Quickly spread fudge in a lightly buttered 8- or 9-inch square pan. Cool.

About 3 dozen squares
Ivy Gene Hamby Winnon

PEANUT BUTTER FUDGE

2 12-oz bags butterscotch morsels

1 28-oz jar of crunchy peanut butter

2 14-oz cans of sweetened condensed milk

Melt first 2 ingredients over medium heat on stove, stirring often—or 5 minutes in microwave. When melted, stir in milk. Mix well. Spray 13x9-inch pan with Pam: pour in mixture. Refrigerate until firm.

Makes 100 1-inch squares
Jacque Winnon Burchfield

EASY PEANUT BUTTER FUDGE

¹/₂ c butter

2 ¹/₄ c brown sugar

¹/₂ c milk

³/₄ c peanut butter

1 tsp vanilla

3 ¹/₂ c powdered sugar

Melt butter in a medium saucepan over medium heat. Stir in brown sugar and milk. Bring to a boil and boil for 2 minutes, stirring frequently. Remove from heat. Stir in peanut butter and vanilla. Then pour mixture over powdered sugar in a large mixing bowl. Beat until smooth, then pour into an 8x8-inch dish or pan. Chill until firm and cut into squares.

I've also tried adding 1 teaspoon of cocoa to the mixture before boiling just to give it a hint of chocolate flavor.

Marilyn S Winnon (Buddy)

> " It's not what you take when you
> leave this world—but what you
> leave behind when you go."

CHOCOLATE–PEANUT BUTTER FUDGE

12 oz pkg chocolate chips	1 tsp vanilla
1 can condensed milk	1 c peanut butter chips

In heavy saucepan, over low heat, melt chocolate chips with condensed milk and vanilla, stirring frequently. Remove from heat. Add peanut butter chips; stir just to distribute chips throughout mixture. Spread evenly into an aluminum-foil-lined 8-inch square pan. Chill 2 hours or until firm. Turn fudge onto cutting board; peel off foil and cut into squares.

Jacque Winnon Burchfield

BUTTERMILK FUDGE
OR PRALINES

2 c sugar	1 c buttermilk
1/2 tsp baking soda	1 tsp vanilla
3 tbsp white corn syrup	2 c pecans
1/2 stick oleo	

Mix all ingredients together, except vanilla and pecans, in large pan. Start on medium-high heat. Stir sides and bottom so it doesn't burn. Boil about 2 minutes then reduce heat to medium low. (If you have a thick boiler there is less danger of candy scorching.) Cook to firm-ball stage. Remove from heat and cool. Add 1 teaspoon vanilla and pecans. Beat until slightly thickened—then drop with spoon on wax paper.

Mae Winnon Mardis

CREOLE PRALINES

3 c sugar	1/2 c nuts
1 c milk	1 tbsp butter
1 tsp vanilla flavor	

Caramelize 1/2 cup sugar. Place sugar milk in heavy boiler. Add caramelized sugar and cook to firm-ball stage. Add butter, flavor, and nuts. Cook 3 minutes. Take off stove and beat until glossy and slightly thick. Drop by teaspoonful on buttered paper or sheet.

Makes 25 small candies
Ivy Gene Winnon

OREO BALLS

1 pkg Oreos
(crush in gallon bag)
1 pkg cream cheese, softened

$^1/_2$ brick white dipping chocolate

Combine ingredients. Place in freezer for approximately 2 hours, remove, and roll into small balls. Melt chocolate in double-boiler. Dip Oreo balls in melted chocolate.

Morgan Watson Johnston

PEANUT BRITTLE

1 $^1/_2$ c sugar
$^1/_2$ c corn syrup
$^1/_2$ c water
dash salt

2 c peanuts
1 tbsp butter
1 tsp baking soda
1 tsp vanilla

Place sugar, syrup, water, salt, and peanuts in 2-quart microwave-proof bowl. Cook on high (max power) 5 minutes, then stir. Cook on high 13–15 minutes or until syrup separates into threads (this is the hard-crack stage) or 300°F on a candy thermometer. Check temperature with thermometer several times in the last few minutes. (Do not leave thermometer in oven while cooking.) Stir in butter, baking soda, and vanilla just until light and bubbly. Pour onto buttered cookie sheet. Spread. Cool and break into pieces.

Jacque Winnon Burchfield

PEANUT BRITTLE

1 c sugar
1 c raw peanuts
$^1/_3$ c Karo syrup

$^1/_3$ c water
pinch salt
1 tsp baking soda

Mix all ingredients except soda. Cook for 15 minutes. Remove from fire and add soda.

Lillian Winnon Atkins

CRACKLE PEANUT BRITTLE

Mrs. Holcomb And Mama's Recipe. This candy was made by these two woman and they enjoyed every minute they were together making it. The candy was enjoyed by all.

2 c sugar

1 c white corn syrup

1 c water (Dolly used
1/2–3/4 cups)

2 c raw peanuts

2 tsp butter

1 tsp baking soda

Stir sugar, syrup, and water over low heat until sugar is dissolved. Then increase heat. Continue cooking until soft ball forms, stirring little. Add peanuts and 1 teaspoon of butter. Cook over heat until it reaches the hard-cracking stage (when you spin mixture off a spoon into a cup of cold water it should become brittle).

Add soda and 1 tsp butter. Pour on greased baking sheet or paper—may also be poured on enamel cabinet top that has been greased well. Butter fingers and pull candy to form thin pieces.

Ivy Gene Hamby Winnon

CROCKPOT CHOCOLATE-PEANUT CLUSTERS

2 lb (2 16-oz jars) dry-roasted peanuts, salted

48 oz almond bark white chocolate

4 oz sweet German chocolate

10–12 oz dark chocolate

Place all ingredients in crockpot. Cook on low for 3 hours.* Don't touch. Turn pot off and let sit for 20 minutes. Cover a large surface (about 3 square feet) with waxed or parchment paper. Stir mixture completely. Drop by iced teaspoonful onto paper. Let harden and store in airtight containers.

> * On the first time making this, you may wish to look at your mixture at 2 hours. If possible try not to lift the lid. The chocolate should look slightly melted and not dry. If it looks okay, continue cooking until 3 hours is reached.

Joan Winnon

PEANUT BUTTER CANDY

1/2 c peanut butter

1 c marshmallows

1 1/2 c Rice Krispies

1 c peanuts

1 pkg almond bark

Melt almond bark. Mix in peanut butter until well blended. Add remaining ingredients. Drop by teaspoon onto wax paper.

Merri (Cissie) Winnon Rushing

"We are never the same after listening to the truth. We may forget it, but we will meet it again."

PEANUT BUTTER RICE KRISPIE TREATS

1 c sugar

1 c Karo syrup

1 c peanut butter

5 c Rice Krispies

Stir sugar, Karo, and peanut butter together while cooking for 5 minutes. Stirring constantly. Stir in Rice Krispies. Put into a buttered cake pan; spread evenly. Cut into squares and serve.

Brenda Winnon Myers

PEANUT BUTTER BALLS

1/2 c oleo, softened

1 box powdered sugar

2 c peanut butter

1 tsp vanilla

1 12-oz pkg chocolate chips

1/2 bar paraffin

Mix oleo, powdered sugar, peanut butter, and vanilla. Roll into small balls. Chill overnight. Melt chocolate chips and paraffin in double boiler. Dip balls in chocolate mixture, then let cool.

Jacque Winnon Burchfield

BUTTERSCOTCH–PEANUT BUTTER CRUNCH

12 oz butterscotch chips

1/2 c crunchy peanut butter

5 c cornflakes

Place cornflakes in a bowl. Melt butterscotch chips and peanut butter. Mix well and pour over cornflakes. Stir and drop onto waxed paper.

Joyce Atkins Keller

PECAN SQUARES

1 yellow cake mix (reserve 2/3 c)

1 stick oleo

1 egg

Put mixture in a greased 9x13-inch pan and bake at 325°F for 15 minutes or until light brown.

FILLING

²/₃ c cake mix

¹/₂ c light brown sugar

1 tsp vanilla

¹/₂ c dark Karo syrup

3 eggs

Mix and pour over cake. Sprinkle on 1 cup chopped pecans. Bake at 325°F for 30 minutes (until it doesn't shake in the middle). DO NOT OVERCOOK.

Jacque Winnon Burchfield

GRANOLA BARS

3 ¹/₂ c quick-cooking oats

1 c chopped almonds

1 egg, beaten

²/₃ c butter, melted

¹/₂ c honey

1 tsp vanilla extract

¹/₂ c sunflower kernels (optional)

¹/₂ c shredded coconut

¹/₂ c dried apples, chopped

¹/₂ c dried cranberries or raisins

¹/₂ c brown sugar, packed

¹/₂ tsp ground cinnamon

Combine oats and almonds in a 15x10-inch baking pan coated with non-stick cooking spray. Bake at 350°F for 15 minutes or until toasted, stirring occasionally.

In a large bowl, combine egg, butter, honey and vanilla. Stir in sunflower kernels, coconut, apples, cranberries or raisins, brown sugar and cinnamon. Stir in oat mixture. Press into a 15x10-inch baking pan coated with non-stick cooking spray. Bake at 350°F for 13–18 minutes or until edges are lightly browned. Cool and cut into bars. Store in an airtight container.

Joyce Atkins Keller

SPICE BARS

³/₄ c oil

¹/₄ c honey

1 c sugar

1 egg

¹/₂ c chopped pecans

2 c flour

¹/₄ tsp salt

1 tsp cinnamon

1 tsp baking soda

Sift flour, salt, cinnamon, and soda together. Add to oil, honey, sugar, and egg mixture. Add chopped pecans. Press into a 9x13-inch lightly greased pan. Bake at 350°F for 15–20 minutes. While warm, ice with icing.

ICING

1/2 c powdered sugar

2 tsp Miracle Whip

1 1/2–2 tsp water
(make thick cream)

Mix together and ice cake. Cut into bars.

Jamie Winnon Rawls

S'MORES

1/3 c light corn syrup

1 pkg milk chocolate chips
or 1/4 c chocolate fudge
frosting mix

1/2 tsp vanilla

1 1/2 c miniature marshmallows

1 tbsp butter or margarine

4 c Golden Grahams cereal

Butter a 9x9x2-inch square pan. Heat corn syrup and butter to boiling in 3-quart saucepan. Remove from heat. Add chocolate chips or frosting mix and vanilla; stir until chocolate is melted or frosting mix is dissolved. Fold in cereal gradually until completely coated with chocolate. Fold in marshmallows. Turn cereal mixture into pan; press with buttered back of spoon. Let stand at room temperature at least one hour. Cut into bars.

Lillian Winnon Atkins

TRASH

1 c condensed milk

12 oz chocolate chips

1/2 bag mini-marshmallows
(2 1/2 c)

1 1/2 c pecans, chopped

1/2 box raisins

Mix condensed milk and chocolate chips and melt over medium heat. Then add pecans, raisins, and marshmallows. Drop on wax paper.

Jacque Winnon Burchfield

MELT-IN-YOUR-MOUTH TOFFEE

1 lb butter

1 c white sugar

2 c semi-sweet chocolate chips
(use the minis), melted

1 c packed brown sugar

1 c chopped walnuts

Put nuts into a 9x13-inch pan. Pour melted chocolate over it.

In a heavy saucepan, combine butter and white and brown sugar. Cook over medium heat, stirring constantly, until mixture boils. Cook to brittle stage (300°F). Remove from heat.

Pour hot mixture over the nuts and chocolate. Let the mixture cool, then flip it over and let the chocolate set. Break into pieces and serve.

Terri Winnon

MILKY WAY ICE CREAM

8 Milky Way bars

1 large can evaporated milk

Melt together and cool slightly.

6 eggs
1 c sugar
1 can condensed milk

1/2 tsp vanilla
1 large can evaporated milk

Mix above ingredients. Stir in Milky Way mixture and fill with milk to fill up 4-quart freezer. Freeze.

Jacque Winnon Burchfield

FRENCH VANILLA ICE CREAM

1 box French vanilla instant pudding
1 gal 2% milk
1 can condensed milk
2 large cans Pet milk

vanilla flavoring, to taste

3/4 c sugar
dash of salt

Mix all ingredients in an ice cream freezer, using enough milk to reach fill line of freezer. Prepare according to freezer instructions.

Yield: 12 Servings
Jacque Winnon Burchfield

SPICED HOT TEA

1/3 c instant tea
1 env lemonade mix
1/8 tsp cloves

1/2 c Tang
1/4 tsp cinnamon
1/3 c sugar

Combine ingredients to make dry mix. Use 2–3 teaspoon dry mix for each cup of boiling water.

Lillian Winnon Atkins

Mocha Mix

2 c coffee creamer
2 c powdered milk
1/4 c instant coffee

2 c sugar
1 c cocoa

Blend all ingredients. Store in airtight jar. To use, place 2 rounded teaspoonfuls in a cup of boiling water.

Mae Winnon Mardis

Punch

1 46-oz can orange juice
1 46-oz can pineapple juice
6 c sugar

1 1-oz container citric acid
2 gal water

Mix well and chill. Add any color food color desired.

Jamie Winnon Rawls

Party Punch

2 pkg strawberry Jell-O

1 c sugar

2 c boiling water
2 large cans pineapple juice

2 large cans frozen orange juice, diluted with 2 cans water
2 large cans frozen lemonade, diluted with 2 cans water
1 can pink lemonade
1 bottle Grenadine (optional)

Mix Jell-O, sugar, and water and cool. Then add rest of ingredients.

Jamie Winnon Rawls

Aunt Vera's Punch

1 large can frozen orange juice, mixed with 3 cans water
1 can frozen lemon juice or lemonade, mixed by directions on can

1 large can pineapple juice

1 box Jell-O gelatin (cherry or strawberry)

Mix all ingredients together and sweeten to taste. Freeze until slushy. May add 1 large bottle of ginger ale prior to serving.

This punch was made by our aunt and always kept in her freezer. When Brenda and I were under the weather we could expect this punch frozen in ice cube form. She always would bring enough so we would enjoy it for days.

Donna Winnon Cox

INDEX

A

Adell's Deluxe Pound Cake 137
Almond Pound Cake, Sour Cream- 139
Amazin' Raisin Cake 139
Apple, and Cheddar Salad, Beet, 31
Apple Brown Betty 178
Apple Cake, Fresh 123
Apple Dapple Cake 123
Apple Dip 13
Apple Enchiladas 179
Apple Pie, French 161
Arm Roast, Barbecued 67
Artichoke, Spinach-, Dip 13
Art's Bread Pudding with Vanilla Sauce 177
Au Gratin Potato Soup 24
Aunt Beattie's "Scratch Cake" 127
Aunt Vera's Chicken Spaghetti 50
Aunt Vera's Pound Cake 137
Aunt Vera's Punch 192
Avocado-Tomato Salad 31

B

Babo's Chicken Spaghetti 49
Baked Beans, Ted's 97
Baked Chicken Salad Pie 37
Baked Pineapple 172
Baked Rice 107
Banana Bread 111
Banana Bread, Debi Brown's 111
Banana Caramel Pie 163
Banana Coconut Cake 124
Banana Pudding, Old Fashion 176
Banana Split Dessert 162
Barbecue, Chuck Roast 67
Barbecued Arm Roast 67
Barbecue Sauce 40
Bar-B-Que Brisket 65
Barry's Brownies 152
Bars
   Granola Bars 189
   Spice Bars 189
Bars, Magic Cookie 157
Basic Cream Pie 168
Beajay's Meal-in-One Cornbread 80
Beans
   3-Bean Soup 21
   Green Bean Wrap 101
   Green String Beans 100
   Kim's Beans 101
   Layered Bean Dip 8
   Louisiana Red Beans And Rice 107
   Ted's Baked Beans 97
   Tonia's Turnip Greens and Bean Soup 26
Beef
   Bar-B-Que Brisket 65
   Big Pot of Stew 68
Beef and Pepper Rice Skillet 67
Beef (ground)
   Brenda's Quick Dish 76
   Cabbage and Beef Soup 22
   Cocktail Meatballs 16
   Corn Bread Pie 75
   Dirty Rice 70
   Enchilada Casserole 71
   Enchiladas 71
   Greek Eggplant with Meat 100
   Hamburger Helper 76
   Hot Tamales 73
   Jamie's Hot Dog Chili 82
   Kim's Beans 101
   Lillian's Meat Loaf 76
   Meatballs and Spaghetti Sauce 76
   Meatball Stew, Texas 68
   Meat Bun Bake 78
   Mexican Quiche 70
   Mexican Stack-Ups 74
   Natchitoches Meat Pies 77
   Pistolettes 75
   Pizza Meat Loaf 77
   Polish Mistakes 18
   Porcupine Meatballs 70
   Ranch Style Chili 69
   Sanchiladas 72
   Tacos 74
   Taco Salad 35
   Taco Soup 25, 26
   Texas-Style Lasagna 72
   Upside-Down Pie 79
Beef Jerky Marinade 41
Beef (roast)
   Barbecued Arm Roast 67
   Chuck Roast Barbecue 67
Beef (steak)
   Kansas City Plaza III Soup 23
   Pepper Steak 65
   Round Steak Casserole 66
   Sliced Beef and Spaghetti 66
Beef, Sunday Roast 65
Beet, Apple, and Cheddar Salad 31
Beets, Pickled 4
Best-Ever Lemon Pie 169
Betty Boo's Creole Bread Pudding 177

Big Pot of Stew 68
Birthday Cake Frosting 150
Biscuits, Cheese 109
Biscuits, Cheesy Sausage 110
Biscuits, Quick Cheese 109
Bisque, Seafood Cream 90
Black-Eyed Cornbread 118
Blueberry Cake 125
Blueberry Cream Cheese Pie 161
Blueberry Dessert 125
Blueberry Muffins, Old-Fashion 113
Blueberry Pie 162
Blue Cheese Salad Dressing 40
Bobby and Steve's Fried Fish 95
Boiled Cookies 156
Bourbon-Chocolate-Pecan Pie 173
Bread-and-Butter Pickles 5
Bread, Dipping Oil for Italian
    13
Bread Pudding, Art's 177
Bread Pudding, Betty Boo's Creole 177
Bread Pudding, White Chocolate 176
Breakfast Bake, Thanksgiving Leftover 64
Breakfast Casserole 79
Brenda's Quick Dish 76
Brisket, Bar-B-Que 65
Broccoli Casserole 97
Broccoli Casserole, Chicken- 47
Broccoli Salad 31
Broccoli Soup 21
Broccoli Toss, Cauliflower- 32
Brownie Delight 153
Brownies, Barry's 152
Brownies, Butterscotch 152
Brownies, Caramel 152
Brownies, Ruth's 153
Brownies, White 153
Buffalo Chicken Wing Dip 8
Buffalo Wings 63
Bundt Cake, German Chocolate 146
Bundt Cake, Lemon- 133
Bundt Cake, Triple-Chocolate 150
Burritos, Chicken 53
Butterfinger Chocolate Chip Cake 144
Butterfinger Dessert 126
Buttermilk Fudge 185
Buttermilk Pie, Dolly's 161
Butter Rum Cake 125
Butterscotch Brownies 152
Butterscotch-Peanut Butter Crunch 188
Buttery Ham and Cheese Sandwiches 83

C
Cabbage and Beef Soup 22
Cabbage Patties, Italian 98
Cabbage, Smothered 98
Cajun Chicken 60
Cajun/Creole (cuisine)
  Betty Boo's Creole Bread Pudding 177
  Cajun Chicken 60
    Cajun Étouffée 61
    Chicken and Sausage Gumbo 59
    Fried Shrimp 88
    Gumbo 58
    Jamie's Seafood Gumbo 89
    Jamie's Shrimp Jambalaya 88
    Pistolettes 75
    Sausage-Shrimp Jambalaya 88
    Seafood Gumbo 90
    Shrimp and Sausage Creole 87
    Shrimp Étoufée 91
    Team Roping Gumbo 59
Cajun Étouffée 61
California Potatoes Casserole 104
Canadian Cheese Soup 22
Candied Sweet Potatoes 106
Candy
    Butterscotch-Peanut Butter Crunch 188
    Divinity 182
    Hard Cinnamon Candy 181
    Marshmallow Cream Divinity 182
    Peanut Brittle 186
    Peanut Butter 187
Caramel Brownies 152
Caramel Cake 126
Caramel Hawaiian Salad 28
Caramel-Nut Pound Cake 138
Caramel Pie, Banana 163
Caramel Rolls 115
Carrot Cake 126
Carrots, Glazed 98
Cauliflower 98
Cauliflower-Broccoli Toss 32
Cheddar Salad, Beet, Apple, and 31
Cheese Ball 14
  Jamie's 15
  Word of Grace 14
Cheese Biscuits 109
Cheese Biscuits, Quick 109
Cheese Bread 110, 111
Cheese, Cream Sauce with 41
Cheese Sauce for Vegetables 42
Cheese Soup, Canadian
    22
Cheesy Chicken and Spaghetti 50
Cheesy Sausage Biscuits 110
Cheesy Scalloped Potatoes 105
Cherry Salad 28
Chess Pie 164
Chex Party Mix 19
Chicken
    Baked Chicken Salad Pie 37
    Buffalo Chicken Wing Dip 8
    Buffalo Wings 63
    Cajun 60
    Cajun Étouffée 61
    Casserole 45, 46
    Chicken-Broccoli Casserole 47
    Chicken Salad 36
    Cornbread Dressing 119

Cornish Hens 63
Gumbo 58
King Ranch Casserole 45
Light King Ranch Chicken Casserole 45
Moroccan Tagine 62
Southern Fried 58
Team Roping Gumbo 59
Chicken and Dumplings 55
Mrs. Bobbie's 56
Chicken Breasts
Creamy Baked 57
Italian Stuffed 57
Parmesan 57
Ritz Cracker 57
Chicken-Broccoli Casserole 47
Chicken Burritos 53
Chicken Casserole 45, 46
Chicken Divan, Divine 58
Chicken, Easy Caribbean Jerk 52
Chicken Enchilada Dip 11
Chicken Enchiladas 53
Chicken Enchiladas, Creamy 54
Chicken, Fajita 52
Chicken Marsala Tetrazzini 50
Chicken Mexican Dish 52
Chicken Noodle Soup 22
Chicken Patties, Southern 51
Chicken Pot Pie 47, 48
Chicken Salad 36
Chicken & Spaghetti 49
Chicken & Spaghetti, Aunt Vera's 50
Chicken & Spaghetti, Babo's 49
Chicken & Spaghetti, Cheesy 50
Chicken Spectacular 61
Chili
Mexican Stack-Ups 74
Texas Two-Step Soup in a Jar 26
Chili, Jamie's Hot Dog 82
Chili, Ranch Style 69
Chili Seasoning Mix 69
Chocolate Bundt Cake, German 146
Chocolate Bundt Cake, Triple- 150
Chocolate Chip Cake, Butterfinger 144
Chocolate, Death by 179
Chocolate Dessert 167
Chocolate Fudge Bars 147
Chocolate-Peanut Butter Fudge 185
Chocolate-Peanut Clusters, Crockpot 187
Chocolate-Pecan Pie, Bourbon- 173
Chocolate Pie 164, 165
Chocolate Pie, Iron-Skillet 166
Chocolate Pie, Jamie's 165
Chocolate Pies, Fried 166
Chocolate Toffee Cake 145
Chocolate, White, Bread Pudding 176
Chowder, Seafood Cream 90
Chuck Roast Barbecue 67
Cilantro Dip 10
Cinnamon Candy, Hard 181

Cinnamon Rolls 114
Cocktail Meatballs 16
Cocoa Fudge 184
Coconut Balls 181
Coconut Bread 111
Coconut Cake 127
Coconut Cake, Banana 124
Coconut Cake, Cream of 128
Coconut Custard Pie, Mrs. Cecil's 168
Coconut Pie, French 168
Coconut Pie, Fresh 167
Coconut Pound Cake 127
Coconut-Sour Cream Layer Cake 128
Coffee
Mocha Mix 192
Coffee Cake, Cranberry 129
Coleslaw, Dressing for 40
Corn And Cheese Casserole 99
Cornbread 117
Cornbread, Beajay's Meal-in-One 80
Cornbread, Black-Eyed 118
Cornbread, Crawfish 118
Cornbread Dressing 119
Cornbread, Hot-Water 118
Cornbread, Mama's 117
Cornbread, Mexican 119
Corn Bread Pie 75
Corn Casserole, Easy 99
Corn Casserole, Mexican 99
Corn Casserole, Rice & 108
Corn Dip 10
Corn, Fried 100
Cornish Hens 63
Corn Salad 34
Crab
Gumbo 58
Hot Crab Dip 9
Jamie's Seafood Gumbo 89
Seafood Gumbo 90
Seafood Neuberg 94
Crackers, Party 18
Crackle Peanut Brittle 187
Cranberry Coffee Cake 129
Cranberry Salad 29
Crawfish
Crawfish Dip 11
Jamie's Seafood Gumbo 89
Seafood Cream Chowder (or Bisque) 90
Crawfish Cornbread 118
Crawfish Dip 11
Crawfish Fettuccini 92
Cream Cake, Italian 131
Cream Cheese Pie, Blueberry 161
Cream Chowder, Seafood 90
Cream of Coconut Cake 128
Cream Pie, Basic 168
Cream Sauce with Cheese 41
Creamy Baked Chicken Breasts 57
Creamy Chicken Enchiladas 54

Creamy Wild Rice and Mushroom Soup in a Jar 27
Creole Bread Pudding, Betty Boo's 177
Creole Pralines 185
Crockpot Chocolate-Peanut Clusters 187
Crockpot Dressing 120
Croquettes, Salmon 93
Custard, Egg 175
Custard Pie, Mrs. Cecil's Coconut 168

D

Death by Chocolate 179
Debi Brown's Banana Bread 111
Deer Steaks, Ted's Fried 86
Delicious Ham and Potato Soup 24
Dell's Hawaiian Cake 136
Dill Pickles, Garlic 6
Dinner Rolls, 90-Minute 116
Dipping Oil for Italian Bread 13
Dips
    Apple Dip 13
    Buffalo Chicken Wing Dip 8
    Chicken Enchilada Dip 11
    Cilantro Dip 10
    Corn Dip 10
    Crawfish Dip 11
    Dipping Oil for Italian Bread 13
    Fruit Dip 13
    Hot Crab Dip 9
    Layered Bean Dip 8
    Layered Shrimp Dip 8
    Mexican Dip 9
    Salsa 12
    Salsa Dip 12
    Spinach-Artichoke Dip 13
Dirty Rice 70
Dishpan Cookies 156
Divine Chicken Divan 58
Divinity Candy 182
Divinity, Marshmallow Cream 182
Dolly's Buttermilk Pie 161
Dressing, Cornbread 119
Dressing, Crockpot 120
Dressing for Coleslaw 40
Dressing, Squash 102
Duck and Wild Rice Soup 23
Dump Cake 129
Dumplings 54
    New Orleans 56
Dumplings, Chicken and 55
    Mrs. Bobbie's 56
Dumplings, Pineapple 179

E

Easy Caribbean Jerk Chicken 52
Easy Corn Casserole 99
Easy Peanut Butter Fudge 184
Easy Pulled Pork 81
Egg Custard 175

Eggnog-Pecan Pound Cake 138
Eggplant with Meat, Greek 100
Eggs
    Pickled 6
Enchilada Casserole 71
Enchiladas 71
Enchiladas, Apple 179
Enchiladas, Chicken 53
Enchiladas, Creamy Chicken 54
Enchiladas, Shrimp 93
Étoufée, Shrimp 91
Étouffée, Cajun 61

F

Fajita Chicken 52
Fettuccini, Crawfish 92
Fig Cake 129
Fig Cookies 157
Fig Preserves 3
Fish, Bobby and Steve's Fried 95
Five Pounds of Fudge 183
Four-Chip Fudge 183
Four-Layer Delight Cake 145
French Apple Pie 161
French Coconut Pie 168
French Vanilla Ice Cream 191
Fresh Apple Cake 123
Fresh Coconut Pie 167
Fresh Vegetable Salad 33
Fried Chicken, Southern 58
Fried Chocolate Pies 166
Fried Corn 100
Fried Fish, Bobby and Steve's 95
Fried Fruit Pies 169
Fried Green Tomatoes 102
Fried Salmon 92
Fried Shrimp 88
Fried Turkey 63
Frosting. See also Icing
Frosting, Birthday Cake 150
Frosting, Seven-Minute 151
Frosting, White Mountain 151
Fruit Cake, Ice Box 131
Fruit Dip 13
Fruit Pies, Fried 169
Fruit Salad 27, 28
Fruit Salad, 3- 28
Fudge Bars, Chocolate 147
Fudge, Buttermilk 185
Fudge, Chocolate-Peanut Butter 185
Fudge, Cocoa 184
Fudge, Easy Peanut Butter 184
Fudge, Five Pounds of 183
Fudge, Four-Chip 183
Fudge Icing 151
Fudge, Mama's 182
Fudge, Peanut Butter 184
Fudge Pudding Cake, Hot 147
Funnel Cake 130

G

Garlic Dill Pickles 6
Garlic Grits 122
Georgia Pecan Pie 174
German Chocolate Bundt Cake 146
Glazed Carrots 98
Granola Bars 189
Grape Salad 29
Gravy, Sausage 81
Greek Eggplant with Meat 100
Greek Salad Dressing 40
Green Bean Wrap 101
Green Salad, Layered 33
Green String Beans 100
Green Tomatoes, Fried 102
Green Tomato Soy 7
Grits, Garlic 122
Gumbo 58
   Team Roping 59
Gumbo, Jamie's Seafood 89
Gumbo, Seafood 90

H

Ham
   Delicious Ham and Potato Soup 24
   Ham Roll-Ups 18
   Jezebel Sauce 42
Ham and Cheese Sandwiches, Buttery 83
Ham and Cheese with Potato Crust 84
Hamburger Helper 76
Ham Roll-Ups 18
Ham Salad for Sandwiches 37
Ham Salad Snowball 37
Hard Cinnamon Candy 181
Hash Brown and Porkchop Casserole 83
Hash Brown Casserole 104
Hash Brown Potato Casserole 104
Hash Brown Quiche 85
Hawaiian Bread 113
Hawaiian Cake, Dell's 136
Heavenly Hash Cake 146
Heavenly Salad 29
Hens, Cornish 63
Homemade Rice Pilaf 107
Honey-Glazed Snack Mix 19
Hot Crab Dip 9
Hot Dog Chili, Jamie's 82
Hot Fudge Pudding Cake 147
Hot Pepper Jelly 4
Hot Tamales 73
Hot-Water Cornbread 118
Hush Puppies 121

I

Ice Box Fruit Cake 131
Ice Box Rolls 116
Ice Cream, French Vanilla 191
Ice Cream, Milky Way 191
Icing. See also Frosting
Icing, Fudge 151

Iron-Skillet Chocolate Pie 166
Italian Cabbage Patties 98
Italian Cream Cake 131
Italian Slices, Powdered Sugar 160
Italian Stuffed Chicken Breasts 57

J

Jambalaya, Jamie's Shrimp 88
Jambalaya, Sausage-Shrimp 88
Jamie's Cheese Ball 15
Jamie's Chocolate Pie 165
Jamie's Hot Dog Chili 82
Jamie's Little Pizza 122
Jamie's Seafood Gumbo 89
Jamie's Shrimp Jambalaya 88
Jell-O Cake 132
Jelly
   Fig 3
   Hot Pepper 4
   Mayhaw 4
Jerk Chicken, Easy Caribbean 52
Jezebel Sauce 42

K

Kansas City Plaza III Soup 23
Kim's Beans 101
King Cake 132
King Ranch Casserole 45
King Ranch Chicken Casserole, Light 45

L

Lace Cookies, Lady Bird Johnson's 157
Lady Bird Johnson's Lace Cookies 157
Lasagna, Texas-Style 72
Layered Bean Dip 8
Layered Green Salad 33
Layered Salad, Seven- 34
Layered Salad Supreme 33
Layered Shrimp Dip 8
Lehigh Valley Shrimp Mold 38
Lemonade Pie 171
Lemon-Bundt Cake 133
Lemon Meringue Pie 170
Lemon Pie, Best-Ever 169
Lemon Tea Cakes 156
Light King Ranch Chicken Casserole 45, 47
Lillian's Meat Loaf 76
Lillian's Tea Cakes 154
Lime Pickles 5
Little Smokies 17
Louisiana Red Beans And Rice 107

M

Magic Cookie Bars 157
Mama's Cornbread 117
Mama's Fudge 182
Mama's Old Timey Tea Cakes 155
Mamaw Bea's Tea Cakes 155
Marinade 41
   Beef Jerky 41

Marshmallow Cream Divinity 182
Martha Washington Balls 181
Mayhaw Jelly 4
Meatballs and Spaghetti Sauce 76
Meatballs, Porcupine 70
Meat Bun Bake 78
Meat Loaf, Lillian's 76
Meat Loaf, Pizza 77
Meat Pies, Natchitoches 77
Melt-in-Your-Mouth Toffee 190
Mexican Cornbread 119
Mexican Corn Casserole 99
Mexican Corn Salad 35
Mexican (cuisine)
  Chicken Burritos 53
  Chicken Enchilada Dip 11
  Chicken Enchiladas 53
  Chicken Mexican Dish 52
  Creamy Chicken Enchiladas 54
  Enchilada Casserole 71
  Enchiladas 71
  Fajita Chicken 52
  Hot Tamales 73
  Mexican Corn Salad 35
  Mexican Salad 35
  Salsa 12
  Sanchiladas 72
  Shrimp Enchiladas 93
  Tacos 74
  Taco Salad 35
  Taco Seasoning 74
  Taco Soup 25, 26
  Texas-Style Lasagna 72
  Tex-Mex Rollups 17
Mexican Dip 9
Mexican Quiche 70
Mexican Salad 35
Mexican Stack-Ups 74
Milky Way Ice Cream 191
Millionaire Pie 171
Mississippi Mud Cake 145
Mocha Mix 192
Molasses Cookies 158
Molten Lava Cakes 148
Monkey Bread 115
Moroccan Tagine 62
Mounds Cake 148
Mrs. Bobbie's Chicken and Dumplings 56
Mrs. Cecil's Coconut Custard Pie 168
Mrs. Field's Cookies 158
Mrs. Price Pound Cake 138
Muffins, Old-Fashion Blueberry 113
Mushroom Soup in a Jar, Creamy Wild Rice
    and 27
My Mother's Oven-Baked Potatoes 105

N

Natchitoches Meat Pies 77
New Orleans Dumplings 56
90-Minute Dinner Rolls 116

No-Bake Sweet Potato Pie 175

O

Okra And Tomato 101
Old Fashion Banana Pudding 176
Old-Fashion Blueberry Muffins 113
Old Fashion Tea Cakes 155
Ole Fashion Possum 86
Onion Rings 102
Oogee Gooee Cake 133
Orange-Pineapple Cake 136
Orange Salad, Spinach- 36
Orchard Salad 30
Oreo Balls 186
Oysters
  Jamie's Seafood Gumbo 89

P

Pancakes 109
Parched Peanuts 18
Party Crackers 18
Party Mix, Chex 19
Party Punch 192
Pasta Salad 36
Peach Cobbler 172
Peach Cobbler, Quick 172
Peanut Brittle 186
Peanut Brittle, Crackle 187
Peanut Butter Balls 188
Peanut Butter Candy 187
Peanut Butter Cookie Blossoms 159
Peanut Butter Cookies 158, 159
Peanut Butter Cookies, Sugar-Free 159
Peanut Butter Crunch, Butterscotch- 188
Peanut Butter Fudge 184
Peanut Butter Fudge, Chocolate- 185
Peanut Butter Fudge, Easy 184
Peanut Butter Pie 172
Peanut Butter Rice Krispie Treats 188
Peanut Clusters, Crockpot Chocolate- 187
Peanuts, Parched 18
Pear Preserves 4
Pecan Delight 174
Pecan Pie, Bourbon-Chocolate- 173
Pecan Pie, Georgia 174
Pecan Pie, Southern 173
Pecan Pound Cake, Eggnog- 138
Pecan Rolls 115
Pecan Squares 188
Pecans, Toasted 19
Pecan Tassies 174
Pepper Steak 65
Pesto 42
Pickled Beets 4
Pickled Eggs 6
Pickled Shrimp 7
Pickles
  Beet 4
  Bread-and-Butter 5
  Eggs 6

Garlic Dill 6
Lime 5
Refrigerator 6
Pickles, Bread-and-Butter 5
Pickles, Garlic Dill 6
Pickles, Lime 5
Pineapple, Baked 172
Pineapple Cake 134
Pineapple Cake, 7-Up 137
Pineapple Cake, Orange- 136
Pineapple Dumplings 179
Pineapple Skillet Cake 135
Pineapple Upside-Down Cake 135
Pinecrest School Cafeteria Rolls 116
Pistolettes 75
Pizza, Jamie's Little 122
Pizza Meat Loaf 77
Polish Mistakes 18
Popcorn Balls 16
Poppy Seed Cake 133
Porcupine Meatballs 70
Pork
  Breakfast Casserole 79
  Dirty Rice 70
  Italian Cabbage Patties 98
  Natchitoches Meat Pies 77
  Spam Casserole 85
Porkchop Casserole, Hash Brown and 83
Porkchop Potato Casserole 82
Porkchops and Rice Casserole 82
Porkchops over Rice 83
Pork, Easy Pulled 81
Possum, Ole Fashion 86
Potato Casserole 103
Potato Casserole, Hash Brown 104
Potato Casserole, Porkchop 82
Potatoes
  Cheesy Scalloped Potatoes 105
  Hash Brown Casserole 104
  My Mother's Oven-Baked Potatoes 105
  Twice Baked Stuffed Potatoes 105
Potatoes Casserole, California 104
Potato Salad, White 39
Potato Soup
  Au Gratin 24
  Delicious Ham and 24
Pound Cake
  Coconut 127
Pound Cake, Adell's Deluxe 137
Pound Cake, Aunt Vera's 137
Pound Cake, Caramel-Nut 138
Pound Cake, Eggnog-Pecan 138
Pound Cake, Mrs. Price 138
Pound Cake, Sour Cream-Almond 139
Powdered Sugar Italian Slices 160
Pralines 185
Pralines, Creole 185
Preserves
  Fig 3
  Pear 4

Pudding Cake, Hot Fudge 147
Pulled Pork, Easy 81
Pumpkin Crumble 139
Punch 192
Punch, Aunt Vera's 192
Punch Bowl Cake 134
Punch, Party 192

Q
Quiche, Hash Brown 85
Quiche, Mexican 70
Quick Cheese Biscuits 109
Quick Peach Cobbler 172

R
Raisin Cake, Amazin' 139
Ranch Style Chili 69
Ravishing Rice 108
Red Beans And Rice, Louisiana 107
Red Seafood Sauce 43
Red Velvet Cake 140
Refrigerator Pickles 6
Ribbon Christmas Salad 30
Rice
  Baked 107
  Louisiana Red Beans and 107
  Ravishing Rice 108
  White/Wild Rice Casserole 108
Rice Box Salad 38
Rice Casserole, Porkchops and 82
Rice Casserole, Sausage and 80
Rice & Corn Casserole 108
Rice, Dirty 70
Rice Krispie Treats, Peanut Butter 188
Rice Pilaf
  Homemade 107
Rice Pilaf, Sausage 81
Rice, Porkchops over 83
Ritz Cracker Chicken Breast 56
Roast Barbecue, Chuck 67
Roast, Barbecued Arm 67
Roast Beef, Sunday 65
Rolls
  90-Minute Dinner 116
  Caramel 115
  Cinnamon 114
  Pecan 115
  Pinecrest School Cafeteria 116
Rolls, Ice Box 116
Round Steak Casserole 66
Roux 60
Ruth's Brownies 153

S
Sad Cake 141
Salad Dressing 39
  Blue Cheese 40
  Greek 40
Salmon Croquettes 93
Salmon, Fried 92

Salsa 12
Salsa Dip 12
Sanchiladas 72
Sandwiches, Buttery Ham and Cheese 83
Sandwiches, Ham Salad for 37
Sausage
  Beajay's Meal-in-One Cornbread 80
  Breakfast Casserole 79
  Cajun Étouffée 61
  Cheesy Sausage Biscuits 110
  Dirty Rice 70
  Gumbo 58
  Little Smokies 17
  Mexican Dip 9
  Pistolettes 75
  Sausage Balls 15
  Shrimp and Sausage Creole 87
  Shrimp Casserole 87
  Team Roping Gumbo 59
Sausage and Rice Casserole 80
Sausage Balls 15
Sausage Bread 112
Sausage Casserole 80
Sausage Gravy 81
Sausage Rice Pilaf 81
Sausage-Shrimp Jambalaya 88
Scalloped Potatoes, Cheesy 105
Scratch Cake, Aunt Beattie's 127
Scripture Cake 141
Seafood Cream Chowder (or Bisque) 90
Seafood Gumbo 90
Seafood Gumbo, Jamie's 89
Seafood Neuberg 94
Seafood Sauce 43
Seafood Sauce, Red 43
Seasoning Salt 43
Seven-Layered Salad 34
Seven-Minute Frosting 151
7-Up Cake 141
7-Up Pineapple Cake 137
Sheath Cake 148, 149
Shrimp
  Gumbo 58
  Jamie's Seafood Gumbo 89
  Layered Shrimp Dip 8
  Lehigh Valley Shrimp Mold 38
  Pickled Shrimp 7
  Rice Box Salad 38
  Seafood Gumbo 90
  Seafood Neuberg 94
  Shrimp Ball 15
  Shrimp Spread 13
Shrimp and Sausage Creole 87
Shrimp and Spaghetti 94
Shrimp Ball 15
Shrimp Casserole 87
Shrimp Enchiladas 93
Shrimp Étoufée 91
Shrimp, Fried 88
Shrimp Jambalaya, Jamie's 88

Shrimp Jambalaya, Sausage- 88
Shrimp Salad 38
Shrimp Spread 13
Sliced Beef and Spaghetti 66
Smoked Turkey 64
Smoked Turkey Roll 64
S'mores 190
Smothered Cabbage 98
Snack Mix, Honey-Glazed 19
Sock-It-To-Me Cake 142
Sopapilla Cheesecake 163
Sour Cream-Almond Pound Cake 139
Sour Cream Layer Cake, Coconut- 128
Southern Chicken Patties 51
Southern Fried Chicken 58
Southern Lane Cake 142
Southern Pecan Pie 173
Spaghetti, Aunt Vera's Chicken 50
Spaghetti, Babo's Chicken 49
Spaghetti, Cheesy Chicken and 50
Spaghetti, Chicken & 49
Spaghetti Sauce, Meatballs and 76
Spaghetti, Shrimp and 94
Spaghetti, Sliced Beef and 66
Spam Casserole 85
Spice Bars 189
Spiced Hot Tea 191
Spinach-Artichoke Dip 13
Spinach-Orange Salad 36
Squash Dressing 102
Squash Puppies 122
Steak
  Beef and Pepper Rice Skillet 67
  Pepper Steak 65
  Round Steak Casserole 66
Stew, Big Pot of 68
Stew, Texas Meatball 68
Strawberry Cake 143
Strawberry Pie 175
String Beans, Green 100
Stuffed Potatoes, Twice-Baked 105
Sugar Cookies 160
Sugar-Free Peanut Butter Cookies 159
Sunday Roast Beef 65
Sweet Potato Casserole 106
Sweet Potatoes, Candied 106
Sweet Potato Pie, No-Bake 175

T
Tacos 74
Taco Salad 35
Taco Seasoning 74
Taco Soup 25, 26
Tagine, Moroccan 62
Tamales, Hot 73
Tartar Sauce 43
Tea Cakes 154
  Lillian's 154
  Mama's Old Timey 155
Tea Cakes, Lemon 156

Tea Cakes, Mamaw Bea's 155
Tea Cakes, Old Fashion 155
Team Roping Gumbo 59
Tea, Spiced Hot 191
Ted's Baked Beans 97
Ted's Fried Deer Steaks 86
Texas Meatball Stew 68
Texas-Style Lasagna 72
Texas Two-Step Soup in a Jar 26
Tex-Mex Rollups 17
Thanksgiving Leftover Breakfast Bake 64
3-Bean Soup 21
3-Fruit Salad 28
Toasted Pecans 19
Toffee Cake, Chocolate 145
Toffee, Melt-in-Your-Mouth 190
Tomato Bisque Soup 25
Tomatoes
  Fried Green 102
  Green Tomato Soy 7
Tomato, Okra and 101
Tomato Salad, Avocado- 31
Tomato Soup 24
Tonia's Turnip Greens and Bean Soup 26
Trash 190
Triple-Chocolate Bundt Cake 150
Tuna Casserole 95
Turkey
  Fried 63
  Smoked 64
  Thanksgiving Leftover Breakfast Bake 64

Turkey Roll, Smoked 64
Turnip Greens and Bean Soup, Tonia's 26
Turtle Cake 150
Turtle Trifle 154
Twice Baked Stuffed Potatoes 105
Two-Eggs Cake 143

U
Upside-Down Pie 79

V
Vanilla Ice Cream, French 191
Vegetable Casserole 103
Vegetable Salad, Fresh 33
Vegetables, Cheese Sauce for 42
Venison, Ted's Fried Deer Steaks
    86

W
Watergate Cake 143
White Brownies 153
White Chocolate Bread Pudding 176
White Mountain Frosting 151
White Potato Salad 39
White/Wild Rice Casserole 108
Wild Rice and Mushroom Soup in a Jar,
        Creamy 27
Word of Grace Cheese Ball 14

Z
Zucchini Bread 113

www.ingramcontent.com/pod-product-compliance
Lightning Source LLC
Chambersburg PA
CBHW022127080426
42734CB00006B/267